I0759624

Ultimate POUND CAKES

CLASSIC RECIPE COLLECTION

UPDATED AND EXPANDED EDITION

83 press®

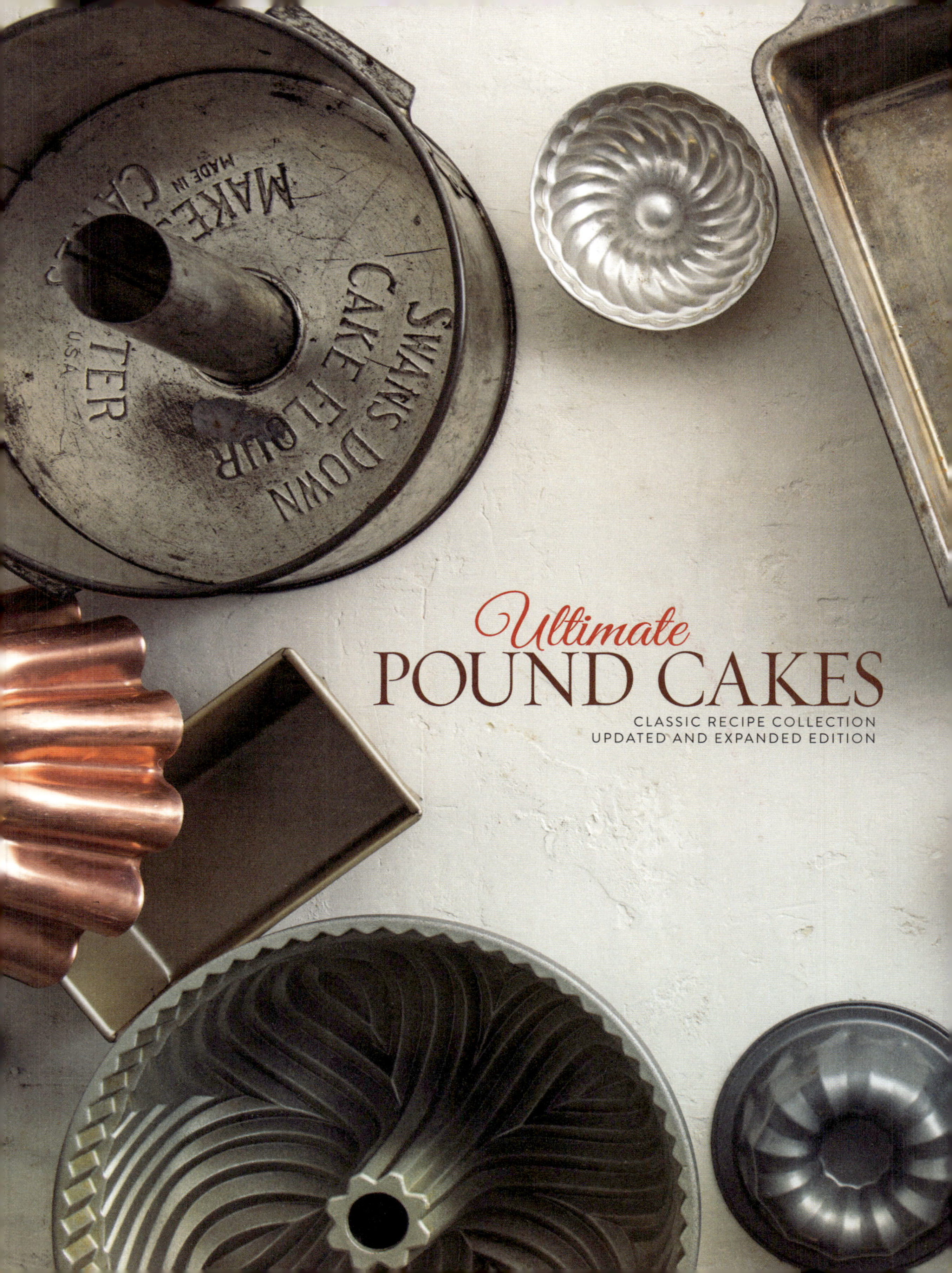

Ultimate POUND CAKES

CLASSIC RECIPE COLLECTION
UPDATED AND EXPANDED EDITION

83 Press
2323 2nd Avenue North
Birmingham, Alabama 35203
83Press.com

ISBN # 979-8-9913469-2-4
Printed in China

ON THE COVER:
Tres Leches Pound Cake, page 55

83
press®

Ultimate Cream Cheese-Vanilla Bean Pound Cake, page 30

contents

foreword

My mother, Phyllis Hoffman DePiano, *loved* pound cake. I think it was not only the sweet buttery taste she adored but the cake's history that grabbed her attention. Pound cake has been handed down through generations dating back to early 18th-century England, when home cooks would take a pound each of flour, eggs, butter, and sugar to fashion a dessert grand enough to feed all the relatives. Whether it was a weeknight supper or holiday celebration, the pound cake always ended a meal with satisfying finesse.

Mom loved to entertain, and when we were growing up, she instilled in my brother Eric and me a love of gatherings with friends and family. We would watch as she cooked everything from mouthwatering appetizers to scrumptious desserts. While Eric gravitated toward savory fare, I was always drawn to baking. As my passion grew, I explored on my travels, often seeking out some of the best bakeries in the world. As an adult, I honed my skills, experimenting and creating, and eventually founded a magazine dedicated to baking, *Bake from Scratch*. But I still have fond memories of Mom's pound cake that was unlike any other. Those comforting pound cakes could take me back to childhood with the first bite.

Mom loved to take the dense crumb of basic pound cake and see what flavors she could add, often consulting with our company's test kitchen on new flavor ideas and how to best incorporate them. After she passed away in 2023, my brother and I discovered dozens of her handwritten recipe cards, including several for pound cakes. Over the years, some of the flavor notes from those cards appeared in our magazines, from *Louisiana Cookin'* to *Taste of the South*. We decided it would be great to incorporate these recipes in an expanded version of the *Ultimate Pound Cakes* cookbook that completely sold out in 2016. We cherish her memory and feel like this is the best way to preserve her fabulous collection of delicious cakes.

In honor of Mom, we share with you this new version of *Ultimate Pound Cakes: Classic Recipe Collection*. I hope that you will enjoy baking these delectable treats for your own gatherings and perhaps be inspired to create some fresh variations of your own.

Brian

Brian Hart Hoffman,
editor of *Bake from Scratch* magazine and
chief creative officer at Hoffman Media

introduction

The late Phyllis Hoffman DePiano enjoyed many passions from sewing to hosting dinner parties where the grand finale was a magnificent homemade pound cake. An accomplished author of several books, including *Gracious Spaces*, *Monograms & Antique Linens*, *The Entertaining Cookbook*, and the *Tiny Book* series of cookbooks, Phyllis founded Hoffman Media in 1983 as a single mother

working from her Birmingham, Alabama, home. Her innate love for an elegant lifestyle inspired all those around her and her business. Hoffman Media, now run by her sons Brian Hart Hoffman and Eric Hoffman, encompasses 83 Press and numerous special interest brands, including *Bake from Scratch*, *Victoria*, *Taste of the South*, *TeaTime*, *The Cottage Journal*, *Southern Lady*, and *Southern Home*.

Brown Sugar Bundt Cake with Bourbon Cherries, page 103

history of pound cake

Rooted in humble beginnings, the pound cake has risen from its original four-ingredient version to complex, delectable masterpieces worthy of any celebration. We aren't completely sure who made the very first pound cake, but we sure are thankful for them.

This simple yet elegant cake gets its name from the earliest northern European adaptations in the 18th century that used a pound each of flour, eggs, butter, and sugar, which would yield a cake large enough to feed several families. It is no wonder that the scrumptious concoction turned up on holiday tables with recipes passed down for generations. Feeding a large group was often the intention back when the recipe first appeared in print in *The Art of Cookery* by Hannah Glasse in 1747. Baking ingredients were hard to come by, so sharing goods was certainly appealing. Nowadays, we have the luxury of baking half-pound cakes in nearly any flavor we prefer. But our desire for this richly dense, tasty cake has not diminished over the years. Although this recipe has English origins, it has become an unequivocal American classic. Author Amelia Simmons penned the first published pound cake recipe in America in her book, *American Cookery*. Her rendition included rosewater—an ambrosial element that seemed to have been popular during the book's publication in 1796. Other favored additions of that time included spices and liquors like rum.

However, methods and ingredients have changed over time to suit evolving tastes. Along with new ingredients, proportions of the basic ingredients were adjusted to make a smaller, less dense cake. While this basic cake no longer has a pound per ingredient, the name stuck. Through the decades, traditional pound cake has become recognized as a basic cake along with fruitcake, spice cake, sponge cake, and angel food cake. These delightful desserts all form a strong foundation for so many of our modern confections. That strong foundation was enhanced tremendously in the mid-19th century when leavening agents like baking powder were introduced, revolutionizing the baking world. These agents release gas into the batter allowing for a lighter cake. People no longer had to rely on eggs alone as their leavening. Another new kitchen ingredient was shortening—a mixture of lard and butter. The combination of baking powder and shortening definitely diminished the need for one pound each of eggs and butter. The introduction of these convenience products brought about a new class of cakes called composition cakes. These cakes were great for bakers on a budget and didn't take nearly as much time to prepare.

With the addition of these modern ingredients, the world of cake baking was introduced to middle-class America for the very first time. The pound cake became a dessert made year-round, not just at large gatherings. It became popular to serve a slice with whipped cream or fruit. Through the years, the availability of certain additives like almond and vanilla extracts, dried pineapple, chopped nuts, or even lemon-lime soda allowed for pound cakes to expand their flavor profiles and texture. As the recipe moved from England to other countries, each culture added their special touch. In France, chocolate or lemon juice was used while the Mexican renditions included walnuts or raisins. Some early recipes called for cornmeal to replace a portion of the then expensive wheat flour. In more recent times, oil and sour cream have been substituted for butter to create a moister cake.

In this book, you will explore pound cake in its many forms, flavors, and fashions—some you may never have seen. These pages are filled with more than 150 recipes and show a bevy of cake pan options to be enjoyed—tube, Bundt, cast iron, loaf, and more! You will see basic pound cakes with classic, buttery notes and compact crumbs and a wide variety of delicious additives and distinctive, decorative flourishes that make each cake a homemade centerpiece. Fresh local products like figs or citrus add seasonal flair while liqueurs and popular beverages raise the profile to new heights. You'll even find some hybrid cakes that play upon styles such as fruitcake or holiday peppermints. In addition, you'll discover glazes, icings, and toppings galore, from simple sweetened whipped cream to crusty sugars that contribute a unique texture. As pound cake evolved, so too, have the array of toppings and sauces that add to the complexity of the simple crumb, ranging from rich chocolate to lofty caramel drizzles.

Pound cakes continue to be the highlight of holidays and entertaining. They also make fabulous presents as modern-day traditions put the pound cake at the center of gift giving, whether for special occasions or just to cheer a friend. Simply put, this cake transports easily and lasts well when stored properly. Home-baked treats are always a welcome surprise for friends and loved ones. We hope these recipes will inspire you to continue the pound cake's legacy of versatility by giving you the opportunity to expand on texture and taste. In any case, these cakes have a history of being a perennial favorite with home bakers and will look stunning on the sideboard at your next fête.

Grandma's Favorite Pound Cake, page 26

tube cakes

Pound cakes are traditionally baked in straight-sided tube pans. The tube pan is loved for the golden crust it gives to these delicious, moist cakes.

SWANS DOWN
CAKE FLOUR
MAKES BETTER
MADE IN
U.S.A
CAKES

Rum Raisin Pound Cake, page 38

Original Pound Cake

MAKES ABOUT 16 SERVINGS

- 1½ cups unsalted butter, softened
- 2½ cups sugar
- 1 tablespoon cornstarch
- 3 cups all-purpose flour, sifted and divided
- 8 large eggs, divided
- ½ teaspoon vanilla extract
- Garnish: whipped cream, sliced fresh strawberries

Preheat oven to 325°. Spray a 10-inch tube pan with baking spray with flour.

In a large bowl, beat butter, sugar, and cornstarch with a mixer at medium speed until fluffy, 3 to 4 minutes, stopping to scrape sides of bowl. Add 1 cup flour, and beat for 1 minute. Add 4 eggs, and beat for 1 minute. Add remaining 2 cups flour, and beat just until combined. Add remaining 4 eggs, and beat until combined. Stir in vanilla. Spoon batter into prepared pan.

Bake for 1 hour. Increase oven temperature to 350°, and bake 15 minutes more. Let cool in pan for 10 minutes. Remove from pan, and let cool completely on a wire rack. Garnish with whipped cream and strawberries, if desired.

cake tip

Don't open the oven door until your cake has baked for at least three-fourths of the recommended baking time. The rush of cold air that hits the cake when the door is opened could cause the cake to collapse.

Grandma's Favorite Pound Cake

MAKES ABOUT 16 SERVINGS

- 1 cup unsalted butter, softened
- ½ cup butter-flavored shortening
- 3 cups sugar
- 5 large eggs
- 3 cups all-purpose flour
- ½ teaspoon salt
- ½ teaspoon baking powder
- 1 cup whole buttermilk
- 1 teaspoon vanilla extract
- ½ teaspoon almond extract
- ½ teaspoon coconut extract

Preheat oven to 325°. Spray a 10-inch tube pan with baking spray with flour.

In a large bowl, beat butter, shortening, and sugar with a mixer at medium speed until fluffy, 3 to 4 minutes, stopping to scrape sides of bowl. Add eggs, one at a time, beating well after each addition.

In a medium bowl, whisk together flour, salt, and baking powder. In a small bowl, combine buttermilk and extracts.

Reduce mixer speed to low. Gradually add flour mixture to butter mixture alternately with buttermilk mixture, beginning and ending with flour mixture, beating just until combined after each addition. Spoon batter into prepared pan. Tap pan on counter to release any air bubbles.

Bake for 45 minutes. Cover with foil, and bake until a wooden pick inserted near center comes out clean, about 45 minutes more. Let cool in pan for 20 minutes. Remove from pan, and let cool completely on a wire rack. Store in an airtight container at room temperature for up to 3 days.

cake tip

Unless the recipe indicates otherwise, all the ingredients (except buttermilk) should be at room temperature before you begin mixing. Butter and eggs at room temperature will blend together more easily to ensure good results.

Honey Almond Pound Cake

MAKES ABOUT 10 SERVINGS

Cake
- 1 (8-ounce) package cream cheese, softened
- 1½ cups unsalted butter, softened
- 2½ cups sugar
- 3 cups all-purpose flour, divided
- 6 large eggs, divided
- 1 teaspoon almond extract
- Honey Citrus Syrup (recipe follows)
- ⅓ cup honey
- ½ cup toasted sliced almonds

Honey Citrus Syrup
Makes about ⅔ cup
- 1 cup water
- ½ cup sugar
- ½ orange, cut into ¼-inch-thick slices
- ½ lemon, cut into ¼-inch-thick slices
- 1 cinnamon stick
- ¼ cup honey

Preheat oven to 325°. Spray a 12-cup tube pan with baking spray with flour.

Cake: In a large bowl, beat cream cheese and butter with a mixer at medium speed until creamy. Add sugar; beat until fluffy, 3 to 4 minutes, stopping to scrape sides of bowl. Reduce mixer speed to low. Add 1 cup flour, beating until combined. Add 2 eggs, beating just until yellow disappears. Repeat procedure twice with remaining 2 cups flour and remaining 4 eggs. Beat in almond extract. Spoon batter into prepared pan.

Bake until a wooden pick inserted near center comes out clean, 1 hour and 20 minutes to 1 hour and 30 minutes. Using an 8-inch wooden skewer, pierce holes ½ inch apart in warm cake. Slowly pour warm Honey Citrus Syrup over cake, allowing cake to absorb syrup. Let cool in pan for 15 minutes. Remove from pan, and drizzle with honey. Sprinkle with almonds. Let cool completely on a wire rack.

Honey Citrus Syrup: In medium saucepan, bring 1 cup water, sugar, orange slices, lemon slices, and cinnamon stick to boil over medium heat. Reduce heat, and simmer for 30 minutes. Strain mixture into small bowl. Stir in honey, and keep warm.

Ultimate Cream Cheese-Vanilla Bean Pound Cake

MAKES ABOUT 16 SERVINGS

- 1 (8-ounce) package cream cheese, softened
- 1 cup unsalted butter, softened
- 3 cups granulated sugar
- 6 large eggs
- 1 vanilla bean, split lengthwise, seeds scraped and reserved
- 1 tablespoon vanilla extract
- 3½ cups all-purpose flour
- 1 teaspoon baking powder
- ½ teaspoon salt
- 1 cup heavy whipping cream

Garnish: confectioners' sugar

Preheat oven to 325°. Spray a 10-inch tube pan with baking spray with flour.

In the bowl of a stand mixer fitted with the paddle attachment, beat cream cheese and butter at medium speed until creamy. Add granulated sugar; beat until fluffy, 3 to 4 minutes, stopping to scrape sides of bowl. Add eggs, one at a time, beating well after each addition. Beat in vanilla bean seeds and vanilla extract.

In a large bowl, whisk together flour, baking powder, and salt. Reduce mixer speed to low. Gradually add flour mixture to butter mixture alternately with cream, beginning and ending with flour mixture, beating just until combined after each addition. Spoon batter into prepared pan.

Bake until a wooden pick inserted near center comes out clean, 1 hour and 20 minutes to 1 hour and 30 minutes, covering with foil halfway through baking to prevent excess browning, if necessary. Let cool in pan for 10 minutes. Remove from pan, and let cool completely on a wire rack. Garnish with confectioners' sugar, if desired.

Carrot Pound Cake

MAKES ABOUT 12 SERVINGS

Cake
- 1 (8-ounce) package cream cheese, softened
- 1½ cups unsalted butter, softened
- 3 cups sugar
- 3 cups all-purpose flour
- 1 teaspoon ground cinnamon
- 6 large eggs, divided
- 1 teaspoon vanilla extract
- ½ teaspoon lemon extract
- 2 cups shredded carrot
- 1 cup chopped pecans

Lemon Glaze (recipe follows)

Lemon Glaze
Makes about ¾ cup
- ⅔ cup confectioners' sugar
- 1 tablespoon whole milk
- ¼ teaspoon lemon extract

Preheat oven to 325°. Spray a 12-cup tube pan with baking spray with flour.

Cake: In large bowl, beat cream cheese and butter with a mixer at medium speed until creamy. Add sugar; beat until fluffy, 3 to 4 minutes, stopping to scrape sides of bowl.

In a medium bowl, whisk together flour and cinnamon. Reduce mixer speed to low. Add 1 cup flour mixture to butter mixture, beating until combined. Add 2 eggs, beating just until yellow disappears. Repeat procedure twice with remaining 2 cups flour mixture and remaining 4 eggs. Stir in extracts. Fold in carrot and pecans. Spoon batter into prepared pan.

Bake until wooden pick inserted near center comes out clean, about 1 hour and 30 minutes. Let cool in pan for 10 minutes. Remove from pan, and let cool completely on a wire rack. Drizzle cooled cake with Lemon Glaze.

Lemon Glaze: In small bowl, whisk together confectioners' sugar, milk, and lemon extract until smooth.

Buttery Champagne Pound Cake

MAKES ABOUT 16 SERVINGS

Cake
1½ cups unsalted butter, softened
2½ cups sugar
5 large eggs
3½ cups all-purpose flour
½ teaspoon baking powder
¼ teaspoon salt
1¼ cups Champagne, or sparkling wine
Champagne Glaze (recipe follows)
Garnish: fresh raspberries

Champagne Glaze
Makes about 1 cup
1 cup sugar
½ cup unsalted butter
½ cup Champagne, or sparkling wine
¼ cup water

Spray a 10-inch tube pan with baking spray with flour.

Cake: In the bowl of a stand mixer fitted with the paddle attachment, beat butter and sugar at medium speed until fluffy, 3 to 4 minutes, stopping to scrape sides of bowl. Add eggs, one at a time, beating well after each addition.

In a medium bowl, whisk together flour, baking powder, and salt. Reduce mixer speed to low. Gradually add flour mixture to butter mixture alternately with Champagne, beginning and ending with flour mixture, beating just until combined after each addition. Spoon batter into prepared pan.

Place pan in a cold oven. Bake at 325° until a wooden pick inserted near center comes out clean, 1 hour and 10 minutes to 1 hour and 20 minutes, covering with foil halfway through baking to prevent excess browning, if necessary. Let cool in pan for 10 minutes. Using a wooden skewer, poke holes all over top of cake. Gradually pour half of Champagne Glaze over cake. Let stand for 30 minutes. Remove from pan, and gradually pour remaining Champagne Glaze over cake. Let cool completely on a wire rack. Garnish with raspberries, if desired.

Champagne Glaze: In a medium saucepan, combine all ingredients. Bring to a boil over medium-high heat; reduce heat, and simmer for 5 minutes, stirring occasionally. Remove from heat, and let cool to room temperature.

Lemon Cake

MAKES ABOUT 12 SERVINGS

Cake
- 2 cups all-purpose flour
- 1½ cups sugar
- 1 tablespoon baking powder
- ½ teaspoon kosher salt
- ½ cup vegetable oil
- 8 large eggs, separated and room temperature
- 2½ tablespoons lemon zest
- ¼ cup fresh lemon juice
- ¼ cup water
- Lemon Glaze (recipe follows)
- Garnish: lemon slices, lemon peel

Lemon Glaze
- 2 cups confectioners' sugar
- ¼ cup unsalted butter, melted
- ¼ cup fresh lemon juice

Preheat oven to 325°.

Cake: In a large bowl, stir together flour, sugar, baking powder, and salt. In a medium bowl, whisk together oil, egg yolks, zest and juice, and ¼ cup water. Fold oil mixture into flour mixture.

In the bowl of a stand mixer fitted with the whisk attachment, beat egg whites at high speed until stiff peaks form, about 2 minutes. Fold one-third of egg whites into batter. Gently fold in remaining egg whites. Do not overmix. Gently spoon batter to an ungreased removeable bottom angel food cake pan.

Bake until top springs back when lightly touched near center, about 1 hour. Immediately invert pan; let cool completely in pan, about 1 hour and 30 minutes.

Run a knife around edges and center of pan. Remove from pan, and let cool completely on a wire rack. Pour Lemon Glaze over cooled cake. Garnish with lemon slices and peel, if desired.

Lemon Glaze: In a small bowl, whisk together all ingredients until smooth. Use immediately.

Rum Raisin Pound Cake

MAKES ABOUT 16 SERVINGS

Cake
- ½ cup spiced rum
- ½ cup raisins
- ½ cup golden raisins
- 2 cups unsalted butter, softened
- 1 cup granulated sugar
- 1 cup firmly packed brown sugar
- 6 large eggs
- 1 (14-ounce) can sweetened condensed milk
- ½ cup whole milk
- 1 tablespoon vanilla extract
- 4 cups all-purpose flour
- 1½ cups chopped walnuts
- Buttery Rum Sauce (recipe follows)

Buttery Rum Sauce
Makes about 1 cup
- ¾ cup granulated sugar
- 6 tablespoons unsalted butter
- 3 tablespoons spiced rum
- 3 tablespoons water
- ½ cup chopped walnuts

Cake: In a small saucepan, heat rum over medium heat for 5 minutes. Remove from heat; stir in all raisins. Cover and let stand for 30 minutes.

Spray a 10-inch tube pan with baking spray with flour.

In the bowl of a stand mixer fitted with the paddle attachment, beat butter and sugars at medium speed until creamy, 3 to 4 minutes, stopping to scrape sides of bowl. Add eggs, one at a time, beating well after each addition. Stir in condensed milk, whole milk, and vanilla.

Reduce mixer speed to low. Gradually add flour to butter mixture, beating until combined. Stir in raisin mixture and walnuts. Spoon batter into prepared pan.

Place pan in a cold oven. Bake at 300° until a wooden pick inserted near center comes out clean, 1 hour and 30 minutes to 1 hour and 40 minutes, covering with foil halfway through baking to prevent excess browning, if necessary. Let cool in pan for 10 minutes. Remove from pan, and let cool completely on a wire rack. Spoon Buttery Rum Sauce over cake just before serving.

Buttery Rum Sauce: In a small saucepan, bring sugar, butter, rum, and 3 tablespoons water to a boil over medium heat. Boil for 3 minutes; remove from heat, and stir in walnuts.

Chocolate Amaretto
Pound Cake, page 51

Black Forest Pound Cake

MAKES ABOUT 16 SERVINGS

Cake
- 1½ cups unsalted butter, softened
- 1½ cups granulated sugar
- 1 cup firmly packed brown sugar
- 5 large eggs
- 1 tablespoon vanilla extract
- 3 cups all-purpose flour
- ¼ cup Dutch process cocoa powder
- 1 teaspoon baking powder
- ½ teaspoon salt
- 2 (4-ounce) bars semisweet chocolate, chopped
- 1 cup heavy whipping cream
- 1 cup sour cream
- Chocolate Glaze (recipe follows)
- Brandied Cherry Sauce (recipe follows)

Chocolate Glaze
Makes about ¾ cup
- 1 (4-ounce) bar semisweet chocolate, chopped
- ⅓ cup heavy whipping cream

Brandied Cherry Sauce
Makes about 4 cups
- 2 (12-ounce) packages frozen cherries
- ⅓ cup granulated sugar
- ⅓ cup cold water
- 2 tablespoons cornstarch
- 2 tablespoons brandy

Spray a 10-inch tube pan with baking spray with flour.

Cake: In the bowl of a stand mixer fitted with the paddle attachment, beat butter and sugars at medium speed until fluffy, 3 to 4 minutes, stopping to scrape sides of bowl. Add eggs, one at a time, beating well after each addition. Beat in vanilla.

In a large bowl, whisk together flour, cocoa, baking powder, and salt. Reduce mixer speed to low. Gradually add flour mixture to butter mixture, beating until combined.

In a small saucepan, combine chocolate and cream. Cook over medium-low heat, stirring frequently, until chocolate is melted and mixture is smooth. Let cool slightly. Add chocolate mixture to butter mixture, beating until combined. Stir in sour cream. Spoon batter into prepared pan.

Place pan in a cold oven. Bake at 325° until a wooden pick inserted near center comes out clean, 1 hour and 20 minutes to 1 hour and 30 minutes, covering with foil halfway through baking to prevent excess browning, if necessary. Let cool in pan for 10 minutes. Remove from pan, and let cool completely on a wire rack. Drizzle with Chocolate Glaze. Let stand until set, about 20 minutes. Spoon Brandied Cherry Sauce over cake just before serving.

Chocolate Glaze: In a small saucepan, combine chocolate and cream. Cook over medium-low heat, stirring frequently, until chocolate is melted and mixture is smooth.

Brandied Cherry Sauce: In a medium saucepan, combine cherries and sugar.

In a small bowl, whisk together ⅓ cup cold water and cornstarch; add to cherry mixture, stirring to combine. Bring to a boil over medium heat, stirring constantly. Reduce heat, and simmer until mixture is very thick, 5 to 6 minutes. Remove from heat; stir in brandy. Let cool for 15 minutes before serving. Serve warm or cold.

Fresh Peach Pound Cake

MAKES ABOUT 16 SERVINGS

- 1 cup unsalted butter, softened
- 3 cups sugar
- 6 large eggs
- 1 teaspoon vanilla extract
- ¼ teaspoon rum extract
- ½ cup sour cream
- 1 (3-ounce) box peach gelatin
- 3 cups all-purpose flour
- ½ teaspoon salt
- ¼ teaspoon baking soda
- ¼ teaspoon ground cinnamon
- ⅛ teaspoon ground nutmeg
- 2 cups chopped fresh peaches

Preheat oven to 325°. Spray a 10-inch tube pan with baking spray with flour.

In a large bowl, beat butter and sugar with a mixer at medium speed until fluffy, 3 to 4 minutes, stopping to scrape sides of bowl. Add eggs, one at a time, beating well after each addition. Stir in extracts.

In a small bowl, combine sour cream and gelatin. Set aside.

In another large bowl, whisk together flour, salt, baking soda, cinnamon, and nutmeg. Reduce mixer speed to low. Gradually add flour mixture to butter mixture, beating until combined. Fold in sour cream mixture and peaches. Spoon batter into prepared pan.

Bake for 1 hour. Cover loosely with foil, and bake until a wooden pick inserted near center comes out clean, 40 to 50 minutes more. Let cool in pan for 10 minutes. Remove from pan, and let cool completely on a wire rack.

Chocolate Pound Cake

MAKES ABOUT 16 SERVINGS

- 1 cup unsalted butter, softened
- ½ cup all-vegetable shortening
- 3 cups sugar
- 5 large eggs
- 1 tablespoon vanilla extract
- 3 cups all-purpose flour
- 5 tablespoons unsweetened cocoa powder
- ½ teaspoon baking powder
- ½ teaspoon baking soda
- ½ teaspoon salt
- 1 cup whole buttermilk

Preheat oven to 325°. Spray a 10-inch tube pan with baking spray with flour.

In a large bowl, beat butter, shortening, and sugar with a mixer at medium speed until fluffy, 3 to 4 minutes, stopping to scrape sides of bowl. Add eggs, one at a time, beating well after each addition. Beat in vanilla.

In another large bowl, whisk together flour, cocoa, baking powder, baking soda, and salt. Reduce mixer speed to low. Gradually add flour mixture to butter mixture alternately with buttermilk, beginning and ending with flour mixture, beating just until combined after each addition. Spoon batter into prepared pan.

Bake until a wooden pick inserted near center comes out clean, 1 hour and 30 minutes to 1 hour and 45 minutes. Let cool in pan for 15 minutes. Remove from pan, and let cool completely on a wire rack. Store in an airtight container for up to 3 days.

cake tip

Whisking together the dry ingredients distributes the leavenings evenly throughout the cake batter, resulting in a good, even rise.

Cinnamon and Chocolate Swirl Pound Cake

MAKES ABOUT 16 SERVINGS

- 1 (4-ounce) bar semisweet chocolate, chopped
- ⅓ cup confectioners' sugar
- ⅓ cup heavy whipping cream
- 1 tablespoon unsalted butter
- 1 tablespoon light corn syrup
- 1½ cups butter-flavored shortening
- 3 cups granulated sugar
- 1 tablespoon ground cinnamon
- 5 large eggs, room temperature
- 3 cups all-purpose flour
- ½ teaspoon salt
- ½ teaspoon baking powder
- 1 cup whole buttermilk, room temperature
- 1 teaspoon vanilla extract

Preheat oven to 325°. Spray a 10-inch tube pan with baking spray with flour.

In a small bowl, place chocolate. In a small saucepan, bring confectioners' sugar, cream, butter, and corn syrup to a boil over medium-high heat. Pour hot cream mixture over chopped chocolate, whisking until smooth. Set aside.

In a large bowl, beat shortening, granulated sugar, and cinnamon with a mixer at medium speed until fluffy, 3 to 4 minutes, stopping to scrape sides of bowl. Reduce mixer speed to medium. Add eggs, one at a time, beating well after each addition.

In a medium bowl, sift together flour, salt, and baking powder. In a small bowl, combine buttermilk and vanilla. Reduce mixer speed to low. Gradually add flour mixture to shortening mixture alternately with buttermilk mixture, beginning and ending with flour mixture, beating just until combined after each addition. Spoon half of batter into prepared pan. Pour chocolate mixture over batter. Using a knife, swirl chocolate mixture through batter. Spoon remaining batter over chocolate mixture. Tap pan on counter to release any air bubbles.

Bake for about 1 hour and 30 minutes until a wooden pick inserted near center comes out clean, covering with foil halfway through baking to prevent excess browning, if necessary. Let cool in pan for 20 minutes. Remove from pan, and let cool completely on a wire rack. Store in an airtight container at room temperature.

Chocolate Amaretto Pound Cake

MAKES ABOUT 16 SERVINGS

Cake
- 1½ cups unsalted butter, softened
- 3 cups sugar
- 5 large eggs
- ¼ cup almond liqueur
- 2 cups all-purpose flour
- ¾ cup unsweetened cocoa powder
- ½ teaspoon salt
- ½ teaspoon baking powder
- 1 cup semisweet chocolate morsels
- 1 cup sour cream
- Chocolate Amaretto Glaze (recipe follows)
- Candied Almonds (recipe follows)

Chocolate Amaretto Glaze
Makes about ¾ cup
- 1 (4-ounce) bar semisweet chocolate, chopped
- ¼ cup heavy whipping cream
- 2 tablespoons almond liqueur

Candied Almonds
Makes about 1 cup
- 1 cup slivered almonds
- 6 tablespoons sugar
- 1 teaspoon salt

Spray a 10-inch tube pan with baking spray with flour.

Cake: In the bowl of a stand mixer fitted with the paddle attachment, beat butter and sugar at medium speed until fluffy, 3 to 4 minutes, stopping to scrape sides of bowl. Add eggs, one at a time, beating well after each addition. Beat in liqueur.

In a large bowl, whisk together flour, cocoa, salt, and baking powder. Reduce mixer speed to low. Gradually add flour mixture to butter mixture, beating until combined. Stir in chocolate morsels and sour cream. Spoon batter into prepared pan.

Place pan in a cold oven. Bake at 325° until a wooden pick inserted near center comes out clean, 1 hour and 20 minutes to 1 hour and 30 minutes, covering with foil halfway through baking to prevent excess browning, if necessary. Let cool in pan for 10 minutes. Remove from pan, and let cool completely on a wire rack. Drizzle with Chocolate Amaretto Glaze, and top with Candied Almonds before serving.

Chocolate Amaretto Glaze: In a small saucepan, combine chocolate, cream, and liqueur. Cook over medium-low heat, stirring frequently, until chocolate is melted and mixture is smooth.

Candied Almonds: In a large skillet, stir together almonds and sugar. Cook over medium heat, stirring constantly, until sugar is melted and almonds are browned. Spread in a single layer on parchment paper; sprinkle with salt. Let stand until cool, about 30 minutes. Store in an airtight container for up to 2 weeks.

Cinnamon-Orange Pound Cake

MAKES ABOUT 12 SERVINGS

- ¾ cup unsalted butter, softened
- ¾ cup all-vegetable shortening
- 3 cups granulated sugar
- 2 tablespoons orange zest
- 7 large eggs
- 1½ teaspoons vanilla extract
- 3 cups all-purpose flour
- 2 teaspoons ground cinnamon
- ¼ teaspoon salt
- ¾ cup whole milk

Garnish: sifted confectioners' sugar, candied orange slices

Preheat oven to 300°. Spray a 12-cup tube pan with baking spray with flour. Line pan with parchment paper.

In a large bowl, beat butter, shortening, granulated sugar, and zest with a mixer at medium speed until fluffy, 3 to 4 minutes, stopping to scrape sides of bowl. Add eggs, one at a time, beating well after each addition. Beat in vanilla.

In a medium bowl, sift together flour, cinnamon, and salt. Reduce mixer speed to low. Gradually add flour mixture to butter mixture alternately with milk, beginning and ending with flour mixture, beating just until combined after each addition. Spoon batter into prepared pan.

Bake for 1 hour. Cover loosely with foil, and bake until a wooden pick inserted near center comes out clean, 45 to 50 minutes more. Let cool in pan for 15 minutes. Remove from pan, and let cool completely on a wire rack. Garnish with confectioners' sugar and candied orange slices, if desired.

Note: Make candied orange slices at home or look for them at a gourmet food store.

Tres Leches Pound Cake

MAKES ABOUT 16 SERVINGS

- 2 cups unsalted butter, softened
- 3 cups plus 2 tablespoons granulated sugar, divided
- 6 large eggs
- 4½ cups all-purpose flour
- ½ teaspoon salt
- 1 (14-ounce) can sweetened condensed milk
- ½ cup whole milk
- 3 teaspoons vanilla extract, divided
- ¼ cup water
- 1 cup heavy whipping cream

Garnish: confectioners' sugar

Preheat oven to 300°. Spray a 15-cup tube pan with baking spray with flour.

In the bowl of a stand mixer fitted with the paddle attachment, beat butter and 2 cups granulated sugar at medium speed until creamy, 3 to 4 minutes, stopping to scrape sides of bowl. Add eggs, one at a time, beating well after each addition.

In a medium bowl, whisk together flour and salt. In another medium bowl, whisk together condensed milk, whole milk, and 2 teaspoons vanilla. Reduce mixer speed to low. Gradually add flour mixture to butter mixture alternately with milk mixture, beginning and ending with flour mixture, beating just until combined after each addition. Spoon batter into prepared pan.

Bake until a wooden pick inserted near center comes out clean, about 1 hour and 30 minutes.

In a small saucepan, bring ¼ cup water and remaining 1 cup and 2 tablespoons granulated sugar to a boil over medium-high heat. Remove from heat. Gradually whisk in cream and remaining 1 teaspoon vanilla. Let cool completely.

Using a wooden pick or skewer, poke holes in warm cake in pan. Slowly pour 1 cup cream mixture over top of cake in pan. Let cool for 30 minutes. Invert cake onto a wire rack lined with foil. Poke holes in cake, and pour remaining cream mixture over cake. Let cool completely. Invert onto a serving plate, and drizzle with remaining cream mixture in foil. Store in refrigerator for up to 1 week. Garnish with confectioners' sugar, if desired.

bundt cakes

Scalloped pans give a fancy, fluted look to pound cakes. The shape offers a suggestion of each slice width, making it a popular choice among hosts.

Citrus Pound Cake, page 73

Browned Butter and Spiced Pear Cake

MAKES ABOUT 12 SERVINGS

Browned Butter
- ¾ cup unsalted butter

Cake
- 2 tablespoons unsalted butter
- 3 cups thinly sliced peeled Bosc pears (about 3 pears)
- 1¼ teaspoons ground cinnamon, divided
- Browned Butter (recipe above)
- 1¾ cups sugar, divided
- 3 large eggs
- 3 cups all-purpose flour
- 1½ teaspoons baking powder
- ¾ teaspoon baking soda
- ¾ teaspoon salt
- ¼ teaspoon ground ginger
- ¼ teaspoon ground nutmeg
- ¼ teaspoon ground allspice
- 1¼ cups whole buttermilk
- 1½ teaspoons vanilla extract

Browned Butter: In a medium saucepan, melt butter over medium heat. Cook until butter turns a medium-brown color and has a nutty aroma, about 10 minutes. Remove from heat, and let cool to room temperature. Refrigerate, stirring occasionally, until almost firm, about 1 hour.

Cake: In a large skillet, melt butter over medium-high heat. Add pears and ¼ teaspoon cinnamon; cook, turning occasionally, until lightly browned and tender, about 5 minutes. Remove from heat, and let cool completely. Preheat oven to 300°. Spray a 12-cup Bundt pan with baking spray with flour.

In a large bowl, beat Browned Butter and 1½ cups sugar with a mixer at medium speed until fluffy, 3 to 4 minutes, stopping to scrape sides of bowl. Add eggs, one at a time, beating well after each addition.

In a medium bowl, whisk together flour, baking powder, baking soda, salt, ginger, nutmeg, allspice, and remaining 1 teaspoon cinnamon. Reduce mixer speed to low. Gradually add flour mixture to butter mixture alternately with buttermilk, beginning and ending with flour mixture, beating just until combined after each addition. Fold in pears and vanilla. Spoon batter into prepared pan. Tap pan twice on counter to release any air bubbles.

Bake until a wooden pick inserted near center comes out clean, about 1 hour and 5 minutes. Let cool in pan for 10 minutes. Remove from pan. Sprinkle warm cake with remaining ¼ cup sugar. Let cool completely.

Filled with fall spices and coated with granulated sugar, this cake tastes just like a doughnut.

Sour Cream Pound Cake

MAKES ABOUT 16 SERVINGS

- 1¼ cups unsalted butter, softened
- 3 cups granulated sugar
- 6 large eggs
- 1 vanilla bean, split lengthwise, seeds scraped and reserved
- 1 tablespoon vanilla extract
- 3 cups all-purpose flour
- ½ teaspoon baking soda
- ¼ teaspoon salt
- 1 (8-ounce) container sour cream
- Garnish: confectioners' sugar, fresh raspberries, whipped cream

Preheat oven to 325°. Spray a 12-cup Bundt pan with baking spray with flour.

In a large bowl, beat butter and granulated sugar with a mixer at medium speed until fluffy, 3 to 4 minutes, stopping to scrape sides of bowl. Add eggs, one at a time, beating well after each addition. Beat in reserved vanilla bean seeds and vanilla extract.

In a medium bowl, whisk together flour, baking soda, and salt. Reduce mixer speed to low. Gradually add flour mixture to butter mixture, beating just until combined. Stir in sour cream. Spoon batter into prepared pan.

Bake until a wooden pick inserted near center comes out clean, about 1 hour, covering with foil to prevent excess browning, if necessary. Let cool in pan for 10 minutes. Remove from pan, and let cool completely on a wire rack. Garnish with sugar, raspberries and whipped cream, if desired.

Almond-Sour Cream Bundt Cake

MAKES ABOUT 16 SERVINGS

- 1½ cups unsalted butter, softened
- 3 cups granulated sugar
- 6 large eggs
- 1 teaspoon vanilla extract
- 3 cups all-purpose flour
- ½ cup finely ground almonds
- 1 teaspoon lemon zest
- ½ teaspoon baking soda
- 1 (8-ounce) container sour cream

Garnish: confectioners' sugar

Preheat oven to 325°. Spray a 10- to 15-cup Bundt pan with baking spray with flour.

In a large bowl, beat butter and granulated sugar with a mixer at medium speed until fluffy, 3 to 4 minutes, stopping to scrape sides of bowl. Add eggs, one at a time, beating well after each addition. Beat in vanilla.

In a medium bowl, combine flour, almonds, zest, and baking soda. Reduce mixer speed to low. Gradually add flour mixture to butter mixture alternately with sour cream, beginning and ending with flour mixture, beating just until combined after each addition. Spoon batter into prepared pan.

Bake until a wooden pick inserted near center comes out clean, 1 hour to 1 hour and 15 minutes. Let cool in pan for 10 minutes. Remove from pan, and let cool completely on a wire rack. Garnish with confectioners' sugar, if desired.

Delta Pound Cake

MAKES ABOUT 16 SERVINGS

- 1½ cups unsalted butter, softened
- 3 cups granulated sugar
- 7 large eggs
- 3 cups all-purpose flour
- ¼ teaspoon salt
- 1 cup heavy whipping cream
- 1½ teaspoons vanilla extract
- Garnish: sifted confectioners' sugar

Preheat oven to 300°. Spray a 10- to 15-cup Bundt pan with baking spray with flour.

In a large bowl, beat butter and granulated sugar with a mixer at medium speed until fluffy, 3 to 4 minutes, stopping to scrape sides of bowl. Add eggs, one at a time, beating well after each addition.

In a medium bowl, sift together flour and salt. Reduce mixer speed to low. Gradually add flour mixture to butter mixture alternately with cream, beginning and ending with flour mixture, beating just until combined after each addition. Beat in vanilla. Spoon batter into prepared pan.

Bake for 1 hour. Cover loosely with foil, and bake until a wooden pick inserted near center comes out clean, 45 to 55 minutes more. Let cool in pan for 15 minutes. Remove from pan, and let cool completely on a wire rack. Garnish with confectioners' sugar, if desired.

7UP® Bundt Cake

MAKES ABOUT 16 SERVINGS

Cake
- 1½ cups unsalted butter, softened
- 2½ cups sugar
- 5 large eggs, room temperature
- 1 teaspoon lemon zest
- 1 teaspoon lime zest
- 1 teaspoon fresh lemon juice
- 1 teaspoon fresh lime juice
- 3 cups unbleached cake flour
- ½ teaspoon salt
- ¾ cup 7UP soda, room temperature
- Lemon-Lime Glaze (recipe follows)

Lemon-Lime Glaze
Makes about ¾ cup
- 2 cups confectioners' sugar
- 3 tablespoons 7UP soda, room temperature

Preheat oven to 350°. Spray a 10-cup Bundt pan with baking spray with flour.

Cake: In the bowl of a stand mixer fitted with the paddle attachment, beat butter and sugar at medium speed until fluffy, 3 to 4 minutes, stopping to scrape sides of bowl. Add eggs, one at a time, beating well after each addition. Beat in zests and juices.

In a medium bowl, whisk together flour and salt. Gradually add flour mixture to butter mixture in three additions, alternately with soda, beginning and ending with flour mixture, beating just until combined after each addition. Spoon batter into prepared pan. Gently tap pan on counter lined with a kitchen towel about 5 to 6 times to release air bubbles.

Bake until a wooden pick inserted near center comes out clean, 1 hour and 10 minutes, covering with foil to prevent excess browning after 40 minutes. Let cool in pan for 10 minutes. Remove from pan, and let cool completely. Drizzle with Lemon-Lime Glaze.

Lemon-Lime Glaze: In a medium bowl, whisk together confectioners' sugar and soda until smooth. Use immediately.

Almond Poppy Seed Cake

MAKES ABOUT 16 SERVINGS

- 1½ cups unsalted butter, softened
- 1¾ cups sugar
- 5 large eggs, separated
- 2⅔ cups all-purpose flour
- 1 teaspoon baking powder
- 1 teaspoon baking soda
- ½ teaspoon salt
- 1 cup whole buttermilk
- ⅓ cup poppy seeds
- 2 teaspoons almond extract

Preheat oven to 325°. Spray a 10- to 15-cup Bundt pan with baking spray with flour.

In a large bowl, beat butter and sugar with a mixer at medium speed until fluffy, 3 to 4 minutes, stopping to scrape sides of bowl. Add egg yolks, one at a time, beating well after each addition.

In a medium bowl, whisk together flour, baking powder, baking soda, and salt. With mixer at low speed, add flour mixture to butter mixture in thirds, alternately with buttermilk, beginning and ending with flour mixture. Beat until combined. Add poppy seeds and extract, stirring just until combined.

In a medium bowl, beat egg whites with a mixer at high speed until stiff peaks form. Gently fold egg whites into batter. Spoon batter into prepared pan.

Bake until a wooden pick inserted near center comes out clean, about 50 minutes. Let cool in pan for 10 minutes. Remove from pan and let cool completely on a wire rack.

LAIT PUR DE NORMANDIE
ARRIVAGE 2 FOIS PAR JOUR
Le bon lait

Citrus Pound Cake

MAKES ABOUT 10 SERVINGS

Cake
1 cup unsalted butter, softened
3 cups sugar
6 large eggs
3 cups all-purpose flour
½ teaspoon baking soda
1½ teaspoons lemon zest
1½ teaspoons lime zest
1½ teaspoons orange zest
1 cup sour cream
2 tablespoons fresh lemon juice
2 tablespoons fresh lime juice
2 tablespoons fresh orange juice
Citrus Glaze (recipe follows)

Citrus Glaze
Makes about 1 cup
2 cups confectioners' sugar
½ teaspoon lemon zest
½ teaspoon lime zest
½ teaspoon orange zest
¼ cup fresh orange juice

Preheat oven to 325°. Spray a 10-cup Bundt pan with baking spray with flour.

Cake: In a large bowl, beat butter and sugar with a mixer at medium speed until fluffy, 3 to 4 minutes, stopping to scrape sides of bowl. Add eggs, one at a time, beating well after each addition.

In a medium bowl, whisk together flour, baking soda, and zests. Reduce mixer speed to low. Gradually add flour mixture to butter mixture, beating just until combined. Add sour cream and juices, beating until combined. Spoon batter into prepared pan.

Bake until a wooden pick inserted near center comes out clean, 1 hour and 5 minutes to 1 hour and 10 minutes. Let cool in pan for 10 minutes. Remove from pan, and let cool completely on a wire rack. Drizzle with Citrus Glaze.

Citrus Glaze: In a small bowl, whisk together all ingredients until combined. Use immediately.

Lemonade Pound Cake

MAKES ABOUT 12 SERVINGS

Cake
- 1½ cups unsalted butter, softened
- 2 cups sugar
- 5 large eggs
- 2 tablespoons lemon zest
- 3 cups all-purpose flour
- 1 teaspoon baking soda
- 1 teaspoon salt
- ¾ cup frozen lemonade concentrate, thawed
- ½ cup sour cream
- Lemonade Glaze (recipe follows)
- Garnish: fresh lemon slices, fresh mint

Lemonade Glaze
Makes about 1 cup
- ¼ cup heavy whipping cream
- 2 tablespoons frozen lemonade concentrate, thawed
- 2 cups confectioners' sugar

Preheat oven to 325°. Spray a 15-cup Bundt pan with baking spray with flour.

Cake: In a large bowl, beat butter and sugar with a mixer at medium speed until fluffy, 3 to 4 minutes, stopping to scrape sides of bowl. Add eggs, one at a time, beating well after each addition. Add zest, beating to combine.

In a medium bowl, whisk together flour, baking soda, and salt. Reduce mixer speed to low. Gradually add flour mixture to butter mixture alternately with lemonade concentrate and sour cream, beginning and ending with flour mixture, beating just until combined after each addition. Spoon batter into prepared pan.

Bake until a wooden pick inserted near center comes out clean, about 1 hour. Let cool in pan for 10 minutes. Remove from pan, and let cool completely on a wire rack. Drizzle with Lemonade Glaze. Garnish with lemon slices and mint, if desired.

Lemonade Glaze: In a medium bowl, combine cream and lemonade concentrate. Gradually whisk in confectioners' sugar until smooth.

Lime Buttermilk Bundt Cake

MAKES ABOUT 12 SERVINGS

Cake
1½ cups unsalted butter, softened
2 cups sugar
3 large eggs, separated
1 teaspoon vanilla extract
1 tablespoon lime zest (from about 2 limes)
3 cups all-purpose flour
1 teaspoon baking powder
¾ teaspoon salt
½ teaspoon baking soda
1½ cups whole buttermilk
5 tablespoons Lime Syrup (recipe follows)
Lime Glaze (recipe follows)
Garnish: lime zest

Lime Syrup
Makes about ¾ cup
½ cup sugar
2 tablespoons lime zest (from about 4 limes)
½ cup fresh lime juice

Lime Glaze
Makes about 1 cup
2 cups confectioners' sugar
½ cup Lime Syrup (recipe above)

Preheat oven to 325°. Spray a 15-cup Bundt pan with baking spray with flour.

Cake: In a large bowl, beat butter and sugar with a mixer at medium speed until fluffy, 3 to 4 minutes, stopping to scrape sides of bowl. Add egg yolks, one at a time, beating well after each addition. Beat in vanilla and zest.

In a medium bowl, whisk together flour, baking powder, salt, and baking soda. Reduce mixer speed to low. Gradually add flour mixture to butter mixture alternately with buttermilk, beginning and ending with flour mixture, beating just until combined after each addition.

In a medium bowl, beat egg whites with a mixer at medium speed until stiff peaks form. Gently fold egg whites into batter. Spoon batter into prepared pan.

Bake until a wooden pick inserted near center comes out clean, about 1 hour and 10 minutes. Using a wooden skewer, poke holes in cake. Pour 4 tablespoons Lime Syrup over warm cake, and let cool in pan for 10 minutes. Remove cake from pan and let cool completely on wire rack. Brush top of cake with about 1 tablespoon Lime Syrup. Drizzle desired amount of Lime Glaze over cooled cake. Garnish with zest, if desired.

Lime Syrup: In a small bowl, whisk together sugar and zest and juice until sugar is dissolved.

Lime Glaze: In a small bowl, whisk together confectioners' sugar and Lime Syrup until smooth.

Italian Cream Bundt Cake

MAKES ABOUT 12 SERVINGS

- 1½ cups unsalted butter, softened
- 1 (8-ounce) package cream cheese, softened
- 2 cups granulated sugar
- 1 cup firmly packed light brown sugar
- 5 large eggs
- 1 tablespoon vanilla extract
- 3 cups all-purpose flour
- ¾ teaspoon salt
- ½ teaspoon baking powder
- 1 cup finely chopped pecans, toasted
- ¾ cup sweetened flaked coconut, toasted

Garnish: confectioners' sugar

Spray a 15-cup Bundt pan with baking spray with flour.

In a large bowl, beat butter, cream cheese, and sugars with a mixer at medium-high speed until fluffy, 3 to 4 minutes, stopping to scrape sides of bowl. Add eggs, one at a time, beating well after each addition. Beat in vanilla.

In a medium bowl, whisk together flour, salt, and baking powder. Reduce mixer speed to low. Gradually add flour mixture to butter mixture, beating just until combined. Stir in pecans and coconut. Spoon batter into prepared pan.

Place pan in a cold oven. Bake at 300° until a wooden pick inserted near center comes out clean, about 1 hour and 20 minutes. Let cool in pan for 10 minutes. Remove from pan, and let cool completely on a wire rack. Garnish with confectioners' sugar, if desired.

White Chocolate Pound Cake

MAKES ABOUT 16 SERVINGS

1 cup unsalted butter, softened
2 cups granulated sugar
5 large eggs
3 cups all-purpose flour
½ teaspoon baking soda
½ teaspoon baking powder
½ teaspoon salt
1 cup whole buttermilk
2 (4-ounce) bars white chocolate, melted
Garnish: confectioners' sugar

Preheat oven to 300°. Spray a 10-cup Bundt pan with baking spray with flour.

In a large bowl, beat butter and sugar with a mixer at medium speed until fluffy, 3 to 4 minutes, stopping to scrape sides of bowl. Add eggs, one at a time, beating well after each addition.

In another large bowl, whisk together flour, baking soda, baking powder, and salt. Reduce mixer speed to low. Gradually add flour mixture to butter mixture alternately with buttermilk, beginning and ending with flour mixture, beating just until combined after each addition. Stir in melted chocolate. Spoon batter into prepared pan.

Bake until a wooden pick inserted near center comes out clean, about 1 hour and 30 minutes. Let cool in pan for 10 minutes. Remove from pan, and let cool completely on a wire rack. Garnish with confectioners' sugar, if desired.

Toasted Coconut Tres Leches Pound Cake, page 99

Almond-Topped Sour Cream Pound Cake

MAKES ABOUT 12 SERVINGS

Cake
- ¼ cup sliced almonds
- 1½ cups unsalted butter, softened
- 1 cup sugar
- 6 large eggs
- 2 teaspoons almond extract
- 1 teaspoon vanilla extract
- 3 cups all-purpose flour
- ⅛ teaspoon baking soda
- 1 (8-ounce) container sour cream
- Sour Cream Topping (recipe follows), to serve

Sour Cream Topping
- 1 cup sour cream
- 1 cup confectioners' sugar
- 1 teaspoon vanilla extract

Preheat oven to 325°. Spray a 15-cup Bundt pan with baking spray with flour. Sprinkle sliced almonds into bottom of prepared pan.

Cake: In a large bowl, beat butter and sugar with a mixer at medium speed until creamy, 3 to 4 minutes, stopping to scrape sides of bowl. Add eggs, one at a time, beating well after each addition. Beat in extracts.

In a medium bowl, whisk together flour and baking soda. Reduce mixer speed to low. Gradually add flour mixture to butter mixture alternately with sour cream, beginning and ending with flour mixture, beating just until combined after each addition. Spoon batter into prepared pan.

Bake until lightly browned and a wooden pick inserted near center comes out clean, 1 hour and 10 minutes to 1 hour and 20 minutes. Let cool in pan for 10 minutes. Remove from pan and let cool completely on a wire rack. Serve with Sour Cream Topping.

Sour Cream Topping: In a small bowl, whisk together sour cream, confectioners' sugar, and vanilla.

Jam-Swirled Bundt Cake

MAKES ABOUT 16 SERVINGS

Cake

- 1½ cups unsalted butter, softened
- 3 cups sugar
- 6 large eggs
- 2 teaspoons lemon zest
- 1 teaspoon vanilla extract
- 3 cups all-purpose flour
- ½ teaspoon baking soda
- ½ teaspoon salt
- ½ cup sour cream
- ¾ cup seedless strawberry jam, divided
- Liquid red food coloring (optional)
- Lemon Glaze (recipe follows)

Lemon Glaze

- 1 cup confectioners' sugar
- 1 tablespoon whole milk
- 1½ teaspoons fresh lemon juice
- ½ teaspoon vanilla extract

Preheat oven to 350°. Spray a 12-cup Bundt pan with baking spray with flour.

Cake: In the bowl of a stand mixer fitted with the paddle attachment, beat butter and sugar at medium speed until light and fluffy, about 5 minutes. Add eggs, one at a time, beating well after each addition. Beat in lemon zest and vanilla.

In a medium bowl, whisk together flour, baking soda, and salt. Reduce mixer speed to low. Gradually add flour mixture to butter mixture alternately with sour cream, beginning and ending with flour mixture, beating until well combined. Spoon half of batter into prepared pan and tap pan gently on countertop 4 to 5 times to release any air bubbles.

In a small bowl, stir together 3 tablespoons remaining batter, ½ cup jam, and food coloring (if using). Spoon jam mixture over batter within ½ inch from sides of pan. With a knife, gently swirl jam into top of batter. Spoon remaining batter on top of swirled jam.

Bake until a wooden pick inserted near center comes out clean, about 1 hour to 1 hour and 5 minutes, covering with foil after 45 minutes to prevent excess browning, if necessary. Let cool in pan for 15 minutes. Remove from pan and let cool completely on a wire rack. Drizzle Lemon Glaze onto cake; let set for 15 to 20 minutes. Warm remaining ¼ cup jam and spoon on top of cake.

Lemon Glaze: In a small bowl, whisk together confectioners' sugar, milk, lemon juice, and vanilla until smooth.

cake tip

When swirling batter be careful not to touch the sides of the pan.

Banana-Coconut Pound Cake

MAKES ABOUT 16 SERVINGS

Cake

- 1½ cups unsalted butter, softened
- 3 cups sugar
- 6 large eggs
- 3 cups all-purpose flour
- 1½ teaspoons baking powder
- 1 teaspoon salt
- ¾ cup whole milk
- 1½ cups mashed ripe banana
- 1 cup sweetened flaked coconut
- 1 cup chopped walnuts
- 1 tablespoon vanilla extract

Banana Glaze (recipe follows)

Banana Glaze

Makes about 1 cup

- 2 cups confectioners' sugar
- ¼ cup whole milk
- ¼ teaspoon banana extract

Preheat oven to 350°. Spray a 10- to 15-cup Bundt pan with baking spray with flour.

Cake: In a large bowl, beat butter and sugar with a mixer at medium speed until fluffy, 3 to 4 minutes, stopping to scrape sides of bowl. Add eggs, one at a time, beating well after each addition.

In a medium bowl, whisk together flour, baking powder, and salt. Reduce mixer speed to low. Gradually add flour mixture to butter mixture alternately with milk, beginning and ending with flour mixture, beating just until combined after each addition. Add mashed banana, coconut, walnuts, and vanilla, beating until combined. Spoon batter into prepared pan.

Bake until a wooden pick inserted near center comes out clean, 1 hour and 35 minutes to 1 hour and 40 minutes. Let cool in pan for 10 minutes. Remove from pan, and let cool completely on a wire rack. Drizzle with desired amount of Banana Glaze.

Banana Glaze: In a small bowl, whisk together all ingredients until smooth. Use immediately.

Butter Cake with Browned Butter-Strawberry Syrup

MAKES ABOUT 16 SERVINGS

Cake
- 2 cups unsalted butter, softened
- 3 cups sugar
- 4 large eggs, room temperature
- 4 cups all-purpose flour
- 1 teaspoon baking powder
- ¾ teaspoon salt
- 1⅓ cups whole milk
- 1 teaspoon vanilla extract
- Browned Butter-Strawberry Syrup (recipe follows), to serve

Browned Butter-Strawberry Syrup
- 4 cups quartered fresh strawberries
- ¼ teaspoon ground cardamom
- ½ cup sugar
- 1 cup unsalted butter
- ¼ cup light corn syrup

Preheat oven to 325°. Spray a 15-cup Bundt pan with baking spray with flour.

Cake: In a large bowl, beat butter and sugar with a mixer at medium speed until fluffy, 3 to 4 minutes, stopping to scrape sides of bowl. Add eggs, one at a time, beating well after each addition.

In another large bowl, whisk together flour, baking powder, and salt. In a small bowl, stir together milk and vanilla. With mixer at low speed, gradually add flour mixture to butter mixture alternately with milk mixture, beginning and ending with flour mixture, beating just until combined after each addition. Spoon batter into prepared pan.

Bake until a wooden pick inserted near center comes out clean, about 1 hour and 30 minutes. Let cool in pan for 10 minutes. Remove from pan, and let cool completely on wire rack. Serve with Browned Butter-Strawberry Syrup.

Browned Butter-Strawberry Syrup: In a medium bowl, stir together strawberries, cardamom, and sugar. Let stand at room temperature until strawberries have softened and released their juice, about 1 hour. Drain strawberries, reserving ½ cup strawberry juice.

In a medium saucepan, melt butter over medium heat. Cook, stirring frequently, until butter turns a medium-brown color and has a nutty aroma, about 10 minutes. Remove from heat; whisk in corn syrup and reserved ½ cup strawberry juice. Add strawberries; stir to combine.

cake tip

Spoon leftover Browned Butter-Strawberry Syrup over vanilla ice cream for an extra treat.

Orange Pound Cake

MAKES ABOUT 12 SERVINGS

Cake
- 1½ cups unsalted butter, softened
- 1 (8-ounce) package cream cheese, softened
- 3 cups sugar
- 2 tablespoons orange zest
- 6 large eggs
- 1 teaspoon vanilla extract
- 3 cups all-purpose flour
- ½ cup whole milk
- ½ cup chopped pecans, toasted

Cream Cheese Swirl (recipe follows)
Orange Glaze (recipe follows)
Garnish: orange slices

Cream Cheese Swirl
- 1 (8-ounce) package cream cheese, softened
- ½ cup confectioners' sugar
- 2 tablespoons all-purpose flour
- 1 large egg
- 1 teaspoon orange zest

Orange Glaze
- 2 cups confectioners' sugar, sifted
- 2 tablespoons fresh orange juice

Preheat oven to 325°. Spray a 15-cup Bundt pan with baking spray with flour.

Cake: In the bowl of a stand mixer fitted with the paddle attachment, beat butter and cream cheese at medium speed until creamy, about 3 minutes. Add sugar and zest, and beat until fluffy, about 2 minutes. Add eggs, one at a time, beating well after each addition. Beat in vanilla.

Reduce mixer speed to low. Gradually add flour to butter mixture alternately with milk, beginning and ending with flour, beating just until combined after each addition. Stir in pecans.

Spoon half of batter into prepared pan. Spoon Cream Cheese Swirl onto batter, avoiding edges of pan. Top with remaining batter. Using a knife, pull blade back and forth through batter to swirl layers together, being careful not to touch sides of pan. Smooth top with an offset spatula.

Bake until a wooden pick inserted near center comes out clean, about 1 hour and 30 minutes. Let cool in pan for 10 minutes. Remove from pan, and let cool completely on a wire rack. Drizzle Orange Glaze over cooled cake. Garnish with orange slices, if desired.

Cream Cheese Swirl: In a medium bowl, beat cream cheese with a mixer at medium speed until creamy, about 3 minutes. Add confectioners' sugar, flour, egg, and zest, beating until smooth, about 2 minutes. Cover and refrigerate until ready to use.

Orange Glaze: In a small bowl, whisk together confectioners' sugar and orange juice until smooth.

This cake is a beautiful blend of sweet cornbread and buttermilk pound cake.

Vanilla Bean Pound Cake with Honey-Orange Drizzle

MAKES ABOUT 8 SERVINGS

2 tablespoons unsalted butter, softened
¼ cup all-purpose flour

Cake
1 cup unsalted butter, softened
1 cup sugar
1 vanilla bean, split lengthwise, seeds scraped and reserved
3 large eggs
1 cup all-purpose flour
¼ cup stone-ground yellow cornmeal
½ teaspoon baking powder
¼ teaspoon salt
⅓ cup whole buttermilk
3 tablespoons honey
½ teaspoon orange zest
Honey-Orange Drizzle (recipe follows)

Honey-Orange Drizzle
½ cup honey
4 (2-inch) strips orange zest
2 tablespoons fresh orange juice
2 star anise
2 cinnamon sticks

Preheat oven to 300°. Spray a 6- cup Bundt pan with baking spray with flour.

Cake: In a large bowl, beat butter, sugar, and reserved vanilla bean seeds with a mixer at medium speed until creamy, 3 to 4 minutes, stopping to scrape sides of bowl. Add eggs, one at a time, beating well after each addition.

In a medium bowl, whisk together flour, cornmeal, baking powder, and salt. Reduce mixer speed to low. Gradually add flour mixture to butter mixture, beating until combined. Beat in buttermilk, honey, and zest. Spoon batter into prepared pan, smoothing top using an offset spatula.

Bake until a wooden pick inserted near center comes out clean, about 1 hour. Let cool in pan for 10 minutes. Remove from pan, and let cool completely on a wire rack. Pour Honey-Orange Drizzle over cake. Garnish with star anise, if desired.

Honey-Orange Drizzle: In a small saucepan, combine honey, zest and juice, star anise, and cinnamon. Cook over low heat until warm, about 15 minutes. Remove star anise and cinnamon sticks before serving.

Strawberry Swirl Pound Cake

MAKES ABOUT 10 SERVINGS

Cake
- 2 tablespoons cool water
- 1 tablespoon cornstarch
- 1 cup puréed fresh strawberries
- 3 cups plus 3 tablespoons sugar, divided
- 1 cup unsalted butter, softened
- 1 (8-ounce) package cream cheese, softened
- 6 large eggs
- 1 tablespoon orange zest
- 1 tablespoon vanilla extract
- 3½ cups all-purpose flour
- 1 teaspoon baking powder
- 1 teaspoon salt
- 1 cup heavy whipping cream
- Buttermilk-Orange Glaze (recipe follows)
- Fresh strawberries, to serve

Buttermilk-Orange Glaze
Makes about ½ cup
- 1½ cups confectioners' sugar, plus more, as needed
- 2 tablespoons whole buttermilk
- 1 tablespoon orange liqueur

Preheat oven to 325°. Spray a 12- to 15-cup Bundt pan with baking spray with flour.

Cake: In a small bowl, whisk together 2 tablespoons cool water and cornstarch until smooth.

In a small saucepan, stir together cornstarch mixture, strawberry purée, and 3 tablespoons sugar. Bring to a boil over medium-high heat, stirring frequently; boil until mixture is thickened, about 1 minute. Remove from heat, and let cool completely. Set aside.

In a large bowl, beat butter and remaining 3 cups sugar with a mixer at medium speed until fluffy, 3 to 4 minutes, stopping to scrape sides of bowl. Add cream cheese, beating until smooth. Add eggs, one at a time, beating well after each addition. Beat in zest and vanilla.

In a medium bowl, whisk together flour, baking powder, and salt. Reduce mixer speed to low. Gradually add flour mixture to butter mixture alternately with cream, beginning and ending with flour mixture, beating just until combined after each addition.

Spoon one-third of batter into prepared pan. Spoon half of strawberry mixture over batter. Repeat layers, ending with batter. Using a knife, gently swirl layers being careful to not touch sides of pan.

Bake until a wooden pick inserted near center comes out clean, about 1 hour and 15 minutes, covering with foil halfway through baking to prevent excess browning. Let cool in pan for 10 minutes. Remove from pan, and let cool completely on a wire rack. Spoon Buttermilk-Orange Glaze over cake. Serve with strawberries. Store covered at room temperature for up to 5 days.

Buttermilk-Orange Glaze: In a small bowl, whisk together all ingredients until smooth. Whisk in additional confectioners' sugar if a thicker consistency is desired. Use immediately.

Toasted Coconut Tres Leches Pound Cake

MAKES ABOUT 16 SERVINGS

- 1½ cups unsalted butter, softened
- 2½ cups sugar
- 1 tablespoon cornstarch
- 3 cups all-purpose flour, divided
- 8 large eggs, divided
- 1 cup plus additional unsweetened flaked coconut, toasted
- 1 teaspoon coconut extract
- 1 (14-ounce) can sweetened condensed milk
- 1 (6-ounce) can evaporated milk
- 1 cup coconut milk

Preheat oven to 325°. Spray a 15-cup Bundt pan with baking spray with flour.

In a large bowl, beat butter, sugar, and cornstarch with a mixer at medium speed until fluffy, 3 to 4 minutes, stopping to scrape sides of bowl. Add 1½ cups flour and 4 eggs, beating until combined. Add remaining 1½ cups flour and remaining 4 eggs, beating until combined. Beat in 1 cup toasted coconut and coconut extract. Spoon batter into prepared pan.

Bake for 1 hour. Increase oven temperature to 350°, and bake for 15 minutes more.

In a large bowl, combine condensed milk, evaporated milk, and coconut milk. Using a wooden skewer, poke holes in warm cake. Slowly pour milk mixture over cake. Sprinkle with additional toasted coconut. Let cool at room temperature for 1 hour. Refrigerate until chilled before serving. Serve directly from pan. Cover and refrigerate for up to 1 week.

Fresh Apple Cake with Orange-Cream Cheese Swirl and Caramel Glaze

MAKES ABOUT 16 SERVINGS

Cake

- 2¼ cups peeled, cored, and grated Granny Smith apples
- 2 teaspoons fresh lemon juice
- 4½ cups all-purpose flour
- 1¼ cups firmly packed light brown sugar
- 1 cup granulated sugar
- 1 tablespoon ground cinnamon
- 1½ teaspoons baking soda
- 1½ teaspoons ground ginger
- ¾ teaspoon salt
- 5 large eggs, lightly beaten
- 1¾ cups canola oil
- 1½ teaspoons vanilla extract
- Orange-Cream Cheese Swirl (recipe follows)
- Caramel Glaze (recipe follows)

Orange-Cream Cheese Swirl
Makes about 2 cups

- 1 (8-ounce) package cream cheese, softened
- ½ cup confectioners' sugar
- 2 tablespoons all-purpose flour
- 1 large egg
- 1 tablespoon orange zest

Caramel Glaze
Makes about 2¼ cups

- 1½ cups granulated sugar
- ½ cup water
- ½ teaspoon fresh lemon juice
- ¾ cup heavy whipping cream, warmed
- ¼ cup unsalted butter, softened
- 1 cup confectioners' sugar

Preheat oven to 325°. Spray a 15-cup Bundt pan with baking spray with flour.

Cake: In a medium bowl, combine apples and lemon juice. Set aside.

In a large bowl, whisk together flour, sugars, cinnamon, baking soda, ginger, and salt. Make a well in the flour mixture and add eggs, oil, and vanilla. Fold until just combined. Fold in apple mixture.

Spoon half of batter into prepared pan. Spoon Orange-Cream Cheese Swirl over batter, avoiding edges of pan. Top with remaining batter. Using a knife, pull blade back and forth through batter to swirl layers, being careful not to touch sides of pan.

Bake until a wooden pick inserted near center comes out clean, about 1 hour and 15 minutes. Let cool in pan for 20 minutes. Remove from pan, and let cool completely on a wire rack. Drizzle with warm Caramel Glaze.

Orange-Cream Cheese Swirl: In a small bowl, whisk together cream cheese, confectioners' sugar, flour, egg, and zest.

Caramel Glaze: In a medium saucepan, bring granulated sugar, ½ cup water, and lemon juice to a boil over medium-high heat. Cook, without stirring, until mixture turns a light amber color, 10 to 15 minutes. Remove from heat, and carefully whisk in warm cream and butter. (Mixture may boil vigorously.) Let cool completely. Add confectioners' sugar, whisking until smooth. Cover and refrigerate for up to 3 weeks.

This showstopper comes together in a snap. Serve leftover cherries over ice cream or in a cocktail.

Brown Sugar Bundt Cake with Bourbon Cherries

MAKES ABOUT 12 SERVINGS

Cake
- ¾ cup unsalted butter
- 1½ cups firmly packed brown sugar
- 3 large eggs, room temperature
- 1 teaspoon vanilla extract
- 3 cups all-purpose flour
- 1½ teaspoons baking powder
- ¾ teaspoon baking soda
- ¾ teaspoon salt
- ½ teaspoon ground cinnamon
- 1¼ cups whole buttermilk
- Bourbon Cherries (recipe follows)

Bourbon Cherries
- ½ cup granulated sugar
- ½ cup firmly packed brown sugar
- 2 cups bourbon
- 1 pound fresh or frozen pitted cherries

Preheat oven to 300°. Spray a 10- to 12-cup Bundt pan with baking spray with flour.

Cake: In a large bowl, beat butter and brown sugar with a mixer at medium speed until fluffy, 3 to 4 minutes, stopping to scrape sides of bowl. Add eggs, one at a time, beating well after each addition. Beat in vanilla.

In a medium bowl, whisk together flour, baking powder, baking soda, salt, and cinnamon. With mixer at low speed, gradually add flour mixture to butter mixture alternately with buttermilk, beginning and ending with flour mixture, beating just until combined after each addition. Spoon batter into prepared pan, smoothing top with an offset spatula.

Bake until a wooden pick inserted near center comes out clean, about 1 hour and 5 minutes. Let cool in pan for 10 minutes. Remove from pan, and let cool completely on a wire rack. Spoon Bourbon Cherries over cake, and drizzle with cherry syrup.

Bourbon Cherries: In a small saucepan, combine sugars and bourbon. Cook over medium heat until sugar is dissolved, about 3 minutes. Increase heat to medium-high; cook until thickened and reduced, 20 to 30 minutes. Remove from heat; stir in cherries. Store extra cherries, refrigerated, in an airtight container for up to 6 weeks.

Vanilla Bundt Cake with Caramel Sauce

MAKES ABOUT 12 SERVINGS

Cake

- 1½ cups unsalted butter, softened
- 2 cups granulated sugar
- 1 cup firmly packed brown sugar
- 5 large eggs
- 1 tablespoon vanilla extract
- 3 cups all-purpose flour
- 1 teaspoon baking powder
- ½ teaspoon salt
- 1 cup whole milk
- Vanilla-Bourbon Caramel Sauce (recipe follows)

Vanilla-Bourbon Caramel Sauce

Makes about 2 cups

- 2 cups granulated sugar
- ¼ cup water
- ½ cup heavy whipping cream, warmed
- 2 tablespoons bourbon
- 1 teaspoon salt
- ½ teaspoon vanilla extract

Preheat oven to 325°. Spray a 10- to 15-cup Bundt pan with baking spray with flour.

Cake: In a large bowl, beat butter and sugars with a mixer at medium speed until fluffy, 3 to 4 minutes, stopping to scrape sides of bowl. Add eggs, one at a time, beating well after each addition. Beat in vanilla.

In another large bowl, whisk together flour, baking powder, and salt. Reduce mixer speed to low. Gradually add flour mixture to butter mixture alternately with milk, beginning and ending with flour mixture, beating just until combined after each addition. Spoon batter into prepared pan, smoothing top using an offset spatula. Tap pan on counter twice to release air bubbles.

Bake until a wooden pick inserted near center comes out clean, about 1 hour and 5 minutes. Let cool in pan for 10 minutes. Remove from pan, and let cool completely on a wire rack. Drizzle with warm Vanilla-Bourbon Caramel Sauce.

Vanilla-Bourbon Caramel Sauce: In a medium saucepan, place sugar and ¼ cup water, swirling to combine thoroughly. Cook over medium-high heat, without stirring, until mixture is an amber color, 10 to 15 minutes. Remove from heat. Carefully stir in warm cream. (Mixture may boil vigorously.) Stir in bourbon, salt, and vanilla. Let cool in pan for 10 minutes, stirring frequently. Cover and refrigerate for up to 3 weeks.

Cranberry Swirl Bundt Cake

MAKES ABOUT 10 SERVINGS

Cake
- 1½ cups unsalted butter, softened
- 1 cup sour cream
- 3 cups sugar
- 5 large eggs
- 1 egg yolk
- 1 tablespoon orange zest
- 1 teaspoon vanilla extract
- 3¼ cups all-purpose flour
- 1 teaspoon apple pie spice
- ½ teaspoon baking soda
- ¼ teaspoon salt
- ½ cup Whole-Berry Cranberry Sauce (recipe follows)
- Whipping Cream Glaze (recipe follows)

Whole-Berry Cranberry Sauce
Makes about 3½ cups
- 2 (12-ounce) packages fresh cranberries
- 1¾ cups firmly packed brown sugar
- 1 cup orange juice
- ½ cup water
- 1 teaspoon minced fresh ginger
- ½ teaspoon vanilla extract

Whipping Cream Glaze
- 6 tablespoons heavy whipping cream
- ½ teaspoon vanilla extract
- 1¼ cups confectioners' sugar

Preheat oven to 325°. Spray a 12- to 15-cup Bundt pan with baking spray with flour.

Cake: In a large bowl, beat butter and sour cream with a mixer at medium speed until creamy. Add sugar, beating until fluffy, 3 to 4 minutes, stopping to scrape sides of bowl. Add eggs and egg yolk, one at a time, beating well after each addition. Add zest and vanilla, beating until combined.

In a medium bowl, whisk together flour, apple pie spice, baking soda, and salt. Reduce mixer speed to low. Gradually add flour mixture to butter mixture, beating just until combined. Reserve 2 cups batter in a medium bowl. Add Whole-Berry Cranberry Sauce to reserved batter, and stir until combined. Spoon 3 cups plain batter into prepared pan. Add cranberry batter. Top with remaining plain batter. Run a knife through batter to swirl layers, being careful not to touch sides of pan. Gently tap pan on counter to release any air bubbles.

Bake until a wooden pick inserted near center comes out clean, about 1 hour and 15 minutes, covering with foil halfway through baking to prevent excess browning, if necessary. Let cool in pan for 10 minutes. Remove from pan, and let cool completely on a wire rack. Drizzle cake with Whipping Cream Glaze.

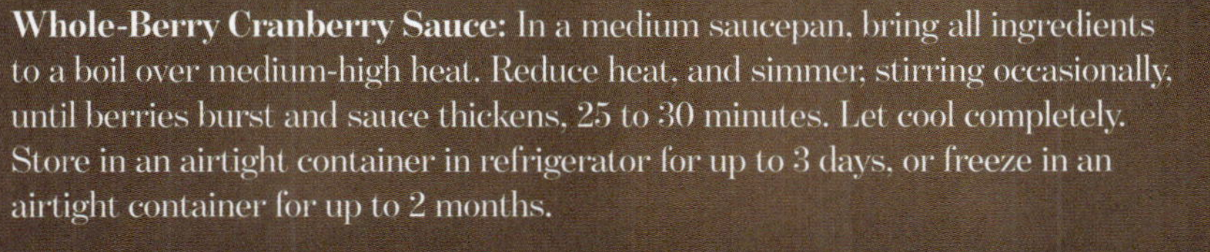

Whole-Berry Cranberry Sauce: In a medium saucepan, bring all ingredients to a boil over medium-high heat. Reduce heat, and simmer, stirring occasionally, until berries burst and sauce thickens, 25 to 30 minutes. Let cool completely. Store in an airtight container in refrigerator for up to 3 days, or freeze in an airtight container for up to 2 months.

Whipping Cream Glaze: In a small bowl, whisk together cream and vanilla. Add confectioners' sugar, whisking until smooth.

Hummingbird Bundt Cake

MAKES ABOUT 16 SERVINGS

Cake
- 2 tablespoons unsalted butter, divided
- 2 cups coarsely chopped fresh pineapple
- 2 cups plus 2 teaspoons sugar, divided
- 3 cups sliced banana (about 4 medium bananas)
- 1 cup canola oil
- 1 teaspoon vanilla extract
- 4 large eggs, room temperature
- 3½ cups all-purpose flour
- 1¼ teaspoons baking soda
- 1 teaspoon ground cinnamon
- ¾ teaspoon salt
- ¼ teaspoon ground nutmeg
- Cream Cheese Glaze (recipe follows)
- Garnish: chopped toasted pecans

Cream Cheese Glaze
Makes about 1 cup
- ¼ cup cream cheese, softened
- 1 tablespoon unsalted butter, softened
- 1½ cups confectioners' sugar
- 1 tablespoon whole milk
- ¼ teaspoon vanilla extract

Preheat oven to 325°. Spray a 15-cup Bundt pan with baking spray with flour.

Cake: In a large skillet, melt 1 tablespoon butter over medium-high heat. Add pineapple and 1 teaspoon sugar. Cook, stirring occasionally, until lightly browned, about 3 minutes. Transfer to a medium bowl. Repeat procedure with remaining 1 tablespoon butter, 1 teaspoon sugar, and banana. Remove from heat; lightly mash banana. Add to pineapple mixture, and let cool for 20 minutes. Stir in oil, vanilla, and eggs.

In a large bowl, stir together flour, baking soda, cinnamon, salt, nutmeg, and remaining 2 cups sugar. Add banana mixture to flour mixture, stirring until combined. Spoon batter into prepared pan.

Bake until a wooden pick inserted near center comes out clean, about 1 hour. Let cool in pan for 10 minutes. Remove from pan, and let cool completely on a wire rack. Spoon Cream Cheese Glaze over cooled cake. Garnish with pecans, if desired.

Cream Cheese Glaze: In a medium bowl, beat cream cheese and butter with a mixer at medium speed until smooth. Gradually add confectioners' sugar, milk, and vanilla, beating until a thick glaze forms.

Pumpkin-Cranberry Bundt Cake

MAKES 8 TO 10 SERVINGS

- ¾ cup dried cranberries, chopped
- ½ cup boiling water
- 2¾ cups self-rising flour
- 1½ teaspoons pumpkin pie spice
- ½ cup unsalted butter, softened
- ½ (8-ounce) package cream cheese, softened
- 1¾ cups firmly packed brown sugar
- 3 large eggs
- 1 cup canned pumpkin
- 2 teaspoons vanilla extract

Garnish: confectioners' sugar

Preheat oven to 350°. Spray a 10-cup Bundt pan with baking spray with flour.

In a small bowl, combine cranberries and ½ cup boiling water; let stand for 10 minutes. Drain.

In a medium bowl, whisk together flour and pumpkin pie spice. Set aside.

In a large bowl, beat butter, cream cheese, and brown sugar with a mixer at medium speed until creamy, 3 to 4 minutes, stopping to scrape sides of bowl. Add eggs, one at a time, beating well after each addition.

Reduce mixer speed to low. Gradually add flour mixture to butter mixture, beating until combined. Beat in cranberries, pumpkin, and vanilla. Spoon batter into prepared pan, smoothing top. Tap pan twice on counter to release air bubbles.

Bake until a wooden pick inserted near center comes out clean, about 45 minutes. Let cool in pan for 15 minutes. Remove from pan, and let cool completely on a wire rack. Garnish with confectioners' sugar, if desired.

cake tip

For an extra delightful treat, serve slices of cake topped with spiced, sweetened whipped cream. In a medium bowl, beat 1 cup heavy whipping cream, 3 tablespoons confectioners' sugar, and ¼ teaspoon pumpkin pie spice with a mixer at high speed until soft peaks form.

Apple cider is reduced
to give this fresh apple cake
a tart yet sweet glaze.

Apple Bundt Cake with Apple Cider Glaze

MAKES ABOUT 12 SERVINGS

Cake

- ¾ cup plus 2 tablespoons unsalted butter, divided
- 3 cups chopped peeled Gala apple (about 3 apples)
- ½ cup apple cider*
- 1½ cups sugar
- 3 large eggs
- 3 cups all-purpose flour
- 1½ teaspoons baking powder
- 1½ teaspoons apple pie spice
- ¾ teaspoon baking soda
- ¾ teaspoon salt
- 1¼ cups whole buttermilk
- 1 teaspoon vanilla extract
- Apple Cider Glaze (recipe follows)
- ⅓ cup chopped toasted pecans

Apple Cider Glaze
Makes about 1 cup

- ¾ cup apple cider*
- 1½ cups confectioners' sugar
- 2 tablespoons heavy whipping cream
- 1 teaspoon unsalted butter, melted
- ⅛ teaspoon salt

Preheat oven to 300°. Spray a 10- to 15-cup Bundt pan with baking spray with flour.

Cake: In a large skillet, melt 2 tablespoons butter over medium-high heat. Add apple; cook, stirring occasionally, until lightly browned and tender, about 4 minutes. Add apple cider; cook until liquid is evaporated. Let cool completely.

In a large bowl, beat sugar and remaining ¾ cup butter with a mixer at medium speed until fluffy, 3 to 4 minutes, stopping to scrape sides of bowl. Add eggs, one at a time, beating well after each addition.

In a medium bowl, whisk together flour, baking powder, apple pie spice, baking soda, and salt. Reduce mixer speed to low. Gradually add flour mixture to butter mixture alternately with buttermilk, beginning and ending with flour mixture, beating just until combined after each addition. Fold in apple and vanilla. Spoon batter into prepared pan, smoothing top using an offset spatula. Tap pan twice on counter to release any air bubbles.

Bake until a wooden pick inserted near center comes out clean, about 1 hour. Let cool in pan for 10 minutes. Remove from pan, and let cool completely on a wire rack. Drizzle Apple Cider Glaze over cake; sprinkle with pecans.

Apple Cider Glaze: In a small saucepan, bring cider to a boil over medium-high heat. Boil until cider reduces to ¼ cup, about 7 minutes. Let cool to room temperature.

In a medium bowl, whisk together reduced cider, confectioners' sugar, cream, melted butter, and salt until smooth.

**We used Martinelli's Sparkling Cider.*

Apple Spice Bundt Cake

MAKES ABOUT 12 SERVINGS

Cake

- 1½ cups unsalted butter, softened
- 1¾ cups sugar
- 3 large eggs
- 3 cups all-purpose flour
- 1 tablespoon apple pie spice
- ½ teaspoon salt
- ½ teaspoon baking powder
- ½ teaspoon baking soda
- 3 cups chopped apple, such as Granny Smith or Gala
- 1 tablespoon vanilla extract
- 2 teaspoons orange zest
- ½ cup chopped pecans
- Brown Sugar Glaze (recipe follows)
- Garnish: Miniature Caramel Apples (see Cake Tip)

Brown Sugar Glaze
Makes about 1 cup

- ½ cup firmly packed brown sugar
- 3 tablespoons apple cider
- 2 tablespoons unsalted butter
- 1 tablespoon dark corn syrup
- ⅛ teaspoon salt
- 1 cup confectioners' sugar

Preheat oven to 325°. Spray a 15-cup Bundt pan with baking spray with flour.

Cake: In a large bowl, beat butter and sugar with a mixer at medium speed until fluffy, 3 to 4 minutes, stopping to scrape sides of bowl. Add eggs, one at a time, beating well after each addition.

In a medium bowl, whisk together flour, apple pie spice, salt, baking powder, and baking soda. Reduce mixer speed to low. Gradually add flour mixture to butter mixture, beating just until combined. Beat in apple, vanilla, and zest. Fold in pecans. (Batter will be thick.) Spoon batter into prepared pan.

Bake until a wooden pick inserted near center comes out clean, about 1 hour and 5 minutes. Let cool in pan for 15 minutes. Remove from pan, and let cool completely on a wire rack. Drizzle with Brown Sugar Glaze. Let stand until glaze is set, about 30 minutes. Garnish with Miniature Caramel Apples, if desired.

Brown Sugar Glaze: In a small saucepan, bring brown sugar, cider, butter, corn syrup, and salt to a boil over medium-high heat. Reduce heat to medium-low; cook for 1 minute. Remove from heat. Add confectioners' sugar; beat with a mixer at low speed for 1 minute. Let cool for 3 minutes before using.

cake tip

To make Miniature Caramel Apples, spray a wire rack with cooking spray. Place rack on a piece of wax paper. Dip Lady apples in Brown Sugar Glaze twice, letting excess drip off. Place on prepared rack, glazed side up. Let stand until set, about 5 minutes.

Lemon-Blueberry Buttermilk Pound Cake

MAKES ABOUT 16 SERVINGS

Cake
- 1 cup unsalted butter, softened
- ½ cup butter-flavored all-vegetable shortening
- 3 cups sugar
- 6 large eggs, room temperature
- 3 cups all-purpose flour
- ½ teaspoon kosher salt
- ½ teaspoon baking powder
- 1 cup whole buttermilk
- 1 tablespoon lemon zest
- 1 tablespoon fresh lemon juice
- 1 teaspoon vanilla extract
- ½ teaspoon almond extract
- ½ teaspoon coconut extract
- 1½ cups fresh blueberries
- Buttermilk Glaze (recipe follows)

Buttermilk Glaze
Makes about 1 cup
- 1½ cups confectioners' sugar
- 2 tablespoons whole buttermilk

Preheat oven to 325°. Spray a 15-cup Bundt pan with baking spray with flour.

Cake: In a large bowl, beat butter and shortening with a mixer at high speed until creamy, about 6 minutes. Reduce mixer speed to medium. Gradually add sugar, beating until fluffy, stopping to scrape sides of bowl. Add eggs, one at a time, beating well after each addition.

In a medium bowl, whisk together flour, salt, and baking powder. In a small bowl, combine buttermilk, zest and juice, and extracts. With mixer at low speed, gradually add flour mixture to butter mixture alternately with buttermilk mixture, beginning and ending with flour mixture, beating just until combined after each addition. Spoon half of batter into prepared pan. Sprinkle blueberries over batter, gently pressing into batter. Spoon remaining batterover blueberries, smoothing top with an offset spatula. Tap pan on counter twice to release air bubbles.

Bake until a wooden pick inserted near center comes out clean, about 1 hour and 10 minutes. Let cool in pan for 10 minutes. Remove from pan, and let cool completely on a wire rack. Drizzle Buttermilk Glaze onto cooled cake.

Buttermilk Glaze: In a medium bowl, whisk together confectioners' sugar and buttermilk until smooth.

cake tip

When baking, allow ingredients like butter, milk, eggs, and cream cheese to come to room temperature before using, unless recipe instructs otherwise.

Apple Butter Pound Cake

MAKES ABOUT 12 SERVINGS

Cake
- 1¼ cups firmly packed brown sugar
- 1 cup apple butter
- ½ cup chopped pecans
- 1½ cups unsalted butter, softened
- 1 (8-ounce) package cream cheese, softened
- 2 cups granulated sugar
- 5 large eggs, room temperature
- 1 tablespoon vanilla extract
- 3 cups all-purpose flour
- 1 teaspoon ground cinnamon
- ¾ teaspoon salt
- ½ teaspoon baking powder
- Brown Sugar Glaze (recipe follows)

Brown Sugar Glaze
Makes about 2 cups
- 1 cup firmly packed light brown sugar
- ⅔ cup heavy whipping cream
- ½ cup unsalted butter
- 1 teaspoon vanilla extract
- ⅛ teaspoon salt
- 1½ cups confectioners' sugar, sifted

Spray a 15-cup Bundt pan with baking spray with flour.

Cake: In a medium bowl, stir together brown sugar, apple butter, and pecans. Set aside.

In a large bowl, beat butter, cream cheese, and granulated sugar with a mixer at medium speed until creamy, 3 to 4 minutes, stopping to scrape sides of bowl. Add eggs, one at a time, beating well after each addition. Beat in vanilla.

In a medium bowl, whisk together flour, cinnamon, salt, and baking powder. Reduce mixer speed to low. Gradually add flour mixture to butter mixture, beating just until combined.

Spoon one-third of batter into prepared pan. Spoon half of apple butter mixture over batter in pan. Top with one-third of batter, remaining apple butter mixture, and remaining batter. Using a knife, pull blade back and forth through batter to swirl layers, being careful to not touch sides of pan. Smooth top using an offset spatula.

Place pan in a cold oven. Bake at 300° until a wooden pick inserted near center comes out clean, about 1 hour and 20 minutes. Let cool in pan for 10 minutes. Remove from pan, and let cool completely on a wire rack. Drizzle with warm Brown Sugar Glaze.

Brown Sugar Glaze: In a medium saucepan, bring brown sugar, cream, butter, vanilla, and salt to a boil over medium-high heat. Cook, stirring constantly, until sugar is dissolved, about 3 minutes. Remove from heat, and let cool for 10 minutes. Whisk in confectioners' sugar. Use immediately or sugar will set.

Pumpkin Bundt Cake with Toffee Sauce

MAKES ABOUT 16 SERVINGS

Cake
- 1 cup unsalted butter, softened
- 2 cups sugar
- 4 large eggs
- 2 teaspoons vanilla extract
- 3 cups all-purpose flour
- 1 tablespoon pumpkin pie spice
- 2 teaspoons baking powder
- 1 teaspoon baking soda
- ½ teaspoon salt
- 1 (15-ounce) can pumpkin

Toffee Sauce (recipe follows)
Garnish: chopped toasted pecans

Toffee Sauce
Makes about 2¼ cups
- 2 cups heavy whipping cream
- 1 cup firmly packed brown sugar
- ¼ cup unsalted butter

Preheat oven to 350°. Spray a 15-cup Bundt pan with baking spray with flour.

Cake: In a large bowl, beat butter and sugar with a mixer at medium speed until fluffy, 3 to 4 minutes, stopping to scrape sides of bowl. Add eggs, one at a time, beating well after each addition. Beat in vanilla.

In a medium bowl, whisk together flour, pumpkin pie spice, baking powder, baking soda, and salt. With mixer at low speed, gradually add flour mixture to butter mixture alternately with pumpkin, beginning and ending with flour mixture, beating just until combined after each addition. Spoon batter into prepared pan.

Bake until a wooden pick inserted near center comes out clean, about 1 hour. Let cool in pan for 20 minutes. Remove from pan and let cool completely on a wire rack. Pour Toffee Sauce over cooled cake. Garnish with pecans, if desired.

Toffee Sauce: In a medium saucepan, bring cream, brown sugar, and butter to a boil over medium-high heat, stirring frequently. Reduce heat to medium-low; simmer until thickened, about 15 minutes. Remove from heat and let cool completely.

Chocolate-Peanut Butter Pound Cake

MAKES ABOUT 12 SERVINGS

Cake
- ½ cup unsalted butter, softened
- ¾ cup creamy peanut butter
- 1 (8-ounce) package cream cheese, softened
- 3 cups sugar
- 6 large eggs
- 1 tablespoon vanilla extract
- 3½ cups all-purpose flour
- 1 teaspoon baking powder
- ½ teaspoon salt
- 1 cup plus 3 tablespoons heavy whipping cream, divided
- ¼ cup unsweetened cocoa powder
- 1 (4-ounce) bar bittersweet chocolate, melted
- Chocolate Glaze (recipe follows)
- Garnish: chopped roasted salted peanuts

Chocolate Glaze
Makes about 1 cup
- 2 (4-ounce) bars semisweet chocolate, chopped
- ¼ cup heavy whipping cream

Preheat oven to 325°. Spray a 12- to 15-cup Bundt pan with baking spray with flour.

Cake: In a large bowl, beat butter, peanut butter, cream cheese, and sugar with a mixer at medium speed until creamy, 3 to 4 minutes, stopping to scrape sides of bowl. Add eggs, one at a time, beating well after each addition. Beat in vanilla.

In a medium bowl, combine flour, baking powder, and salt. Reduce mixer speed to low. Gradually add flour mixture to butter mixture alternately with 1 cup cream, beginning and ending with flour mixture, beating just until combined after each addition. In a medium bowl, reserve 3 cups batter.

To reserved batter, add cocoa and remaining 3 tablespoons cream, stirring until smooth. Stir in melted chocolate. Alternately spoon peanut butter batter and chocolate batter into prepared pan. Gently swirl batters together with a knife.

Bake until a wooden pick inserted near center comes out clean, about 1 hour and 10 minutes. Let cool in pan for 10 minutes. Remove from pan, and let cool completely on a wire rack. Spoon Chocolate Glaze over cake. Cover and refrigerate for up to 3 days. Garnish with chopped peanuts, if desired.

Chocolate Glaze: In a small saucepan, combine chocolate and cream. Cook over low heat, stirring constantly, until chocolate is melted and mixture is smooth. Use immediately.

Mamère's Supermoist Fruitcake

MAKES ABOUT 14 SERVINGS

- 3 cups self-rising flour, divided
- 1 cup raisins
- 1 cup dried cranberries
- 1 cup chopped walnuts
- 8 ounces candied pineapple, coarsely chopped
- 8 ounces packaged pitted dates, coarsely chopped
- 4 ounces candied red cherries
- 4 ounces candied green cherries
- 1½ cups sugar
- 1 cup unsalted butter, melted
- 4 large eggs
- 2 tablespoons ground cinnamon
- ½ teaspoon ground nutmeg
- 1 cup pineapple juice
- ½ cup brandy
- 6 candied red cherries (optional)
- 6 candied green cherries (optional)
- ½ cup brandy or cognac (optional)

Preheat oven to 275°. Spray a 15-cup Bundt pan with baking spray with flour.

In a large bowl, toss together 1 cup flour, raisins, cranberries, walnuts, candied pineapple, dates, 4 ounces red cherries, and 4 ounces green cherries until well coated.

In another large bowl, whisk together sugar, melted butter, and eggs.

In a medium bowl, whisk together cinnamon, nutmeg, and remaining 2 cups flour. Gradually add cinnamon mixture to sugar mixture alternately with pineapple juice, beginning and ending with cinnamon mixture, whisking until combined after each addition and no lumps remain. Add fruit mixture and ½ cup brandy, and fold until well combined. Spoon batter into prepared pan.

Bake for 1 hour and 30 minutes. Gently press 6 red cherries (optional) and 6 green cherries (optional) into top of cake. Bake until a wooden pick inserted near center comes out clean, 30 minutes to 1 hour more. Let cool in pan for 15 minutes. Invert cake onto a wire rack over a rimmed baking sheet. Let cool completely, ladling brandy or cognac (optional) over cake for a spiked flavor. Cover with foil, and refrigerate for up to 7 days.

cake tip

You may wish to bake 4 or 5 of these cakes and offer them as Christmas gifts to family and friends.

Peanut Butter Pound Cake

MAKES ABOUT 16 SERVINGS

- 1 cup unsalted butter, softened
- 1½ cups granulated sugar
- 1 cup firmly packed brown sugar
- ½ cup creamy peanut butter
- 5 large eggs
- 1 teaspoon vanilla extract
- 3 cups all-purpose flour
- ½ teaspoon baking powder
- ¼ teaspoon salt
- 1 cup whole milk
- 1 (10-ounce) package swirled milk chocolate and peanut butter morsels

Garnish: confectioners' sugar, miniature chocolate-covered peanut butter cups

Preheat oven to 325°. Spray a 10- to 15-cup Bundt pan with baking spray with flour.

In a large bowl, beat butter, sugars, and peanut butter with a mixer at medium speed until fluffy, 3 to 4 minutes, stopping to scrape sides of bowl. Add eggs, one at a time, beating well after each addition. Beat in vanilla.

In a medium bowl, whisk together flour, baking powder, and salt. Reduce mixer speed to low. Gradually add flour mixture to butter mixture alternately with milk, beginning and ending with flour mixture, beating just until combined after each addition. Stir in swirled morsels. Spoon batter into prepared pan.

Bake until a wooden pick inserted near center comes out clean, 1 hour and 15 minutes to 1 hour and 25 minutes, covering with foil to prevent excess browning, if necessary. Let cool in pan for 10 minutes. Remove from pan, and let cool completely on a wire rack. Garnish with confectioners' sugar and peanut butter cups, if desired.

Spiced Rum-Pecan Pound Cake

MAKES ABOUT 16 SERVINGS

Cake
- 1 cup unsalted butter, softened
- ½ (8-ounce) package cream cheese, softened
- 1 cup sugar
- 1 cup firmly packed light brown sugar
- 3 large eggs
- 3 cups plus 1 tablespoon all-purpose flour, divided
- 2 teaspoons baking powder
- ½ teaspoon salt
- ¾ cup whole milk
- ¼ cup spiced rum
- 1 teaspoon vanilla extract
- 1 cup chopped pecans, toasted
- Spiked Ambrosia (recipe follows), to serve
- Sweetened whipped cream, to serve

Spiked Ambrosia
- 4 cups orange sections (about 8 large oranges)
- 1 cup sweetened flaked coconut
- ½ cup fresh orange juice
- 2 tablespoons spiced rum

Preheat oven to 325°. Spray a 15-cup Bundt pan with baking spray with flour.

Cake: In a large bowl, beat butter and cream cheese with a mixer at medium speed until creamy. Add sugars, and beat until fluffy, 3 to 4 minutes, stopping to scrape sides of bowl. Add eggs, one at a time, beating well after each addition.

In a medium bowl, whisk together 3 cups flour, baking powder, and salt. In a small bowl, stir together milk, rum, and vanilla. With mixer at low speed, gradually add flour mixture to butter mixture alternately with milk mixture, beginning and ending with flour mixture, beating just until combined after each addition. In a small bowl, toss together pecans and remaining 1 tablespoon flour, shaking off excess. Fold pecans into batter. Spoon batter into prepared pan, smoothing top. Tap pan on counter twice to release air bubbles.

Bake until a wooden pick inserted near center comes out clean, 55 minutes to 1 hour. Let cool in pan for 10 minutes. Remove from pan, and let cool completely on a wire rack. Serve with Spiked Ambrosia and whipped cream.

Spiked Ambrosia: In a medium bowl, combine all ingredients. Refrigerate for at least 30 minutes or up to 3 hours.

Peanut Butter and Honey Pound Cake

MAKES ABOUT 10 SERVINGS

Cake
- 1 cup unsalted butter, softened
- ½ cup creamy peanut butter
- 2 cups sugar
- 5 large eggs
- ½ cup half-and-half
- 1 teaspoon vanilla extract
- 2½ cups all-purpose flour
- ½ teaspoon salt
- 1 (10-ounce) bag peanut butter morsels
- Cream Cheese Glaze (recipe follows)
- Garnish: chopped honey roasted peanuts

Cream Cheese Glaze
- 1 (8-ounce) package cream cheese, softened
- ¼ cup honey
- 2 tablespoons heavy whipping cream

Preheat oven to 300°. Spray a 15-cup Bundt pan with baking spray with flour.

Cake: In a large bowl, beat butter, peanut butter, and sugar with a mixer at medium speed until fluffy, 3 to 4 minutes, stopping to scrape sides of bowl. Add eggs, one at a time, beating well after each addition. Beat in half-and-half and vanilla.

In a medium bowl, whisk together flour and salt. Reduce mixer speed to low. Gradually add flour mixture to butter mixture, beating until combined. Stir in peanut butter morsels. Spoon batter into prepared pan.

Bake until a wooden pick inserted near center comes out clean, 1 hour and 10 minutes to 1 hour and 20 minutes, loosely covering with foil during last 20 minutes of baking to prevent excess browning. Let cool in pan for 10 minutes. Remove from pan, and let cool completely on a wire rack. Drizzle Cream Cheese Glaze over cooled cake. Garnish with peanuts, if desired.

Cream Cheese Glaze: In a small bowl, beat cream cheese, honey, and cream with a mixer at medium speed until smooth.

Green Tomato Bundt Cake

MAKES ABOUT 10 SERVINGS

- 1 cup grated green tomato
- 1 cup finely chopped green tomato
- 1 teaspoon kosher salt, divided
- 2½ cups plus ½ teaspoon all-purpose flour, divided
- 1 cup granulated sugar
- 1 cup firmly packed brown sugar
- 1½ teaspoons apple pie spice
- ½ teaspoon baking powder
- ½ teaspoon baking soda
- ¼ teaspoon ground black pepper
- 1 cup canola oil
- 4 large eggs
- 2 teaspoons vanilla extract
- 1 teaspoon lemon zest
- ½ cup toasted pecans, chopped

Garnish: confectioners' sugar

Preheat oven to 350°. Spray a 12-cup Bundt pan with baking spray with flour.

Place tomato and ¼ teaspoon salt in a colander; let drain for 10 minutes. Pat dry with a paper towel.

In a large bowl, stir together 2½ cups flour, sugars, pie spice, baking powder, baking soda, pepper, and remaining ¾ teaspoon salt. Add oil, eggs, vanilla, and zest. Beat with a mixer at medium speed until combined, stopping occasionally to scrape sides of bowl. In a small bowl, toss together pecans and remaining ½ teaspoon flour. Add to batter, stirring gently to combine. Spoon into prepared pan.

Bake until a wooden pick inserted near center comes out clean, 45 to 50 minutes. Let cool in pan for 10 minutes. Remove from pan, and let cool completely on a wire rack. Garnish with confectioners' sugar, if desired.

Candied Sweet Potato Bundt Cake

MAKES ABOUT 12 SERVINGS

- 1 cup unsalted butter, softened
- 2 cups firmly packed brown sugar
- 1 (16-ounce) can candied yams (sweet potatoes), undrained
- 3 large eggs
- 1 teaspoon vanilla extract
- 3 cups all-purpose flour
- 2 tablespoons baking powder
- 1 teaspoon ground cinnamon
- ¼ teaspoon salt
- ½ cup whole buttermilk
- 1½ cups confectioners' sugar, sifted
- ¼ cup heavy whipping cream

Garnish: praline pecans

Preheat oven to 325°. Spray a 10- to 12-cup Bundt pan with baking spray with flour.

In a large bowl, beat butter and brown sugar with a mixer at medium speed until fluffy, 3 to 4 minutes, stopping to scrape sides of bowl. Beat in yams. Add eggs, one at a time, beating well after each addition. Beat in vanilla.

In a medium bowl, whisk together flour, baking powder, cinnamon, and salt. Reduce mixer speed to low. Gradually add flour mixture to butter mixture alternately with buttermilk, beginning and ending with flour mixture, beating just until combined after each addition. Spoon batter into prepared pan.

Bake until a wooden pick inserted near center comes out clean, 45 to 55 minutes. Let cool in pan 10 minutes. Remove from pan, and let cool completely on a wire rack.

In a small bowl, whisk together confectioners' sugar and cream until smooth. Spoon over cake. Garnish with praline pecans, if desired.

1/2 teaspoon

Brown Sugar Pound Cake

MAKES ABOUT 16 SERVINGS

Cake

- 1½ cups unsalted butter, softened
- 2 cups firmly packed brown sugar
- 1 cup granulated sugar
- 5 large eggs
- 3 cups all-purpose flour
- 1 teaspoon baking powder
- ½ teaspoon salt
- 1 cup whole milk
- 1 (8-ounce) package toffee bits
- 1 cup chopped pecans
- Caramel Drizzle (recipe follows)

Caramel Drizzle

Makes about 1½ cups

- 1 (14-ounce) can sweetened condensed milk
- 1 cup firmly packed brown sugar
- 2 tablespoons unsalted butter
- ½ teaspoon vanilla extract

Preheat oven to 325°. Spray a 12- to 15-cup Bundt pan with baking spray with flour.

Cake: In a large bowl, beat butter and sugars with a mixer at medium speed until fluffy, 3 to 4 minutes, stopping to scrape sides of bowl. Add eggs, one at a time, beating well after each addition.

In a medium bowl, whisk together flour, baking powder, and salt. Reduce mixer speed to low. Gradually add flour mixture to butter mixture alternately with milk, beginning and ending with flour mixture, beating just until combined after each addition. Stir in toffee bits and pecans. Spoon batter into prepared pan.

Bake until a wooden pick inserted near center comes out clean, 1 hour and 15 minutes to 1 hour and 25 minutes, covering with foil to prevent excess browning, if necessary. Let cool in pan for 10 minutes. Remove from pan, and let cool completely on a wire rack. Spoon warm Caramel Drizzle over cooled cake.

Caramel Drizzle: In a medium saucepan, bring condensed milk and brown sugar to a boil over medium-high heat, whisking frequently. Reduce heat, and simmer for about 8 to 9 minutes, whisking frequently. Remove from heat; whisk in butter and vanilla. Let cool for 5 minutes before using.

Pumpkin-Chocolate Swirl Bundt Cake

MAKES ABOUT 12 SERVINGS

- 1 cup unsalted butter, softened and divided
- 1½ cups firmly packed brown sugar
- 3 large eggs
- ½ cup sour cream
- 1 teaspoon vanilla extract
- 3 cups all-purpose flour, divided
- 2 teaspoons baking powder
- 1 teaspoon baking soda
- 1 teaspoon salt
- 1 cup canned pumpkin
- 1½ teaspoons pumpkin pie spice
- ⅓ cup half-and-half
- 2 tablespoons unsweetened cocoa powder
- 2 tablespoons confectioners' sugar

Preheat oven to 300°. Spray a 10- to 15-cup Bundt pan with baking spray with flour.

In a large bowl, beat butter and brown sugar with a mixer at medium speed until fluffy, 3 to 4 minutes, stopping to scrape sides of bowl. Add eggs, one at a time, beating well after each addition. Beat in sour cream and vanilla.

In a medium bowl, whisk together flour, baking powder, baking soda, and salt. Reduce mixer speed to low. Gradually add flour mixture to butter mixture, beating just until combined. Spoon 1 cup vanilla batter into a medium bowl and set aside.

Add pumpkin and pumpkin pie spice to remaining batter; beat until combined. Add half-and-half and cocoa to reserved 1 cup vanilla batter, whisking until combined. (Batters will be thick.)

Spoon one-third of pumpkin batter into prepared pan. Spoon half of chocolate batter by heaping teaspoonfuls over pumpkin batter. Repeat once, spooning remaining pumpkin batter on top. Gently swirl batters together with a knife, being careful to not touch sides of pan. Tap pan twice on counter to release any air bubbles.

Bake until a wooden pick inserted near center comes out clean, 55 minutes to 1 hour. Let cool in pan for 10 minutes. Remove from pan, and let cool completely on a wire rack. Dust with confectioners' sugar.

Pumpkin adds sweetness and tenderness to this marbled Bundt cake.

Strawberry Almond Cake

MAKES ABOUT 16 SERVINGS

- 1 cup unsalted butter, softened
- 2⅔ cups granulated sugar
- 4 large eggs
- ½ teaspoon almond extract
- 3 cups all-purpose flour
- 1 cup almond flour*
- 4 teaspoons baking powder
- ½ teaspoon salt
- 1⅔ cups whole buttermilk
- 2 cups diced fresh strawberries
- ½ cup sliced almonds

Garnish: confectioners' sugar

Preheat oven to 350°. Spray a 16-cup cast-iron fluted cake pan with baking spray with flour.

In the bowl of a stand mixer fitted with the paddle attachment, beat butter and granulated sugar at medium speed until fluffy, 3 to 4 minutes, stopping to scrape sides of bowl. Add eggs, one at a time, beating well after each addition. Beat in extract.

In a medium bowl, whisk together flours, baking powder, and salt. With mixer at low speed, gradually add flour mixture to butter mixture alternately with buttermilk, beginning and ending with flour mixture, beating just until combined after each addition. Fold strawberries into batter.

Sprinkle bottom and sides of prepared pan with sliced almonds. Spoon batter into pan. Gently tap pan on counter to release air bubbles.

Bake until a wooden pick inserted near center comes out clean, about 1 hour and 10 minutes. Let cool in pan on a wire rack for 15 minutes. Removed cake from pan onto wire rack, and let cool completely. Garnish with confectioners' sugar, if desired.

**We used King Arthur Blanched & Super Finely Ground Almond Flour.*

Easy Cinnamon Swirl Bundt Cake

MAKES 10 SERVINGS

Cake
- 1½ cups firmly packed light brown sugar, divided
- Spice Blend (recipe follows)
- 1½ cups unsalted butter, softened
- 1½ cups granulated sugar
- 4 large eggs
- 2 teaspoons vanilla extract
- 4 cups all-purpose flour
- 2½ teaspoons baking powder
- ½ teaspoon salt
- 1½ cups sour cream
- Sugar Glaze (recipe follows)

Spice Blend
Makes about 2 tablespoons
- 2 teaspoons ground cinnamon
- 2 teaspoons ground cardamom
- 1 teaspoon ground cloves
- 1 teaspoon ground ginger
- ½ teaspoon ground white pepper

Sugar Glaze
- 2 cups confectioners' sugar
- 3 tablespoons whole milk
- 2 tablespoons light corn syrup

Preheat oven to 325°. Spray a 15-cup Bundt pan with baking spray with flour.

Cake: In a small bowl, stir together ½ cup brown sugar and Spice Blend. Set aside.

In the bowl of a stand mixer fitted with the paddle attachment, beat butter, granulated sugar, and remaining 1 cup brown sugar at medium speed until fluffy, 3 to 4 minutes, stopping to scrape sides of bowl. Add eggs, one at a time, beating well after each addition. Beat in vanilla.

In a large bowl, whisk together flour, baking powder, and salt. Reduce speed of mixer to low. Gradually add flour mixture to butter mixture alternately with sour cream, beginning and ending with flour mixture, beating just until combined after each addition.

Spoon one-third of batter into prepared pan. Sprinkle with half of sugar-spice mixture. Repeat procedure 1 time; top with remaining one-third of batter. Using a knife, swirl layers of batter and sugar-spice mixture, being sure to not touch sides of pan.

Bake until a wooden pick inserted near center comes out clean, about 1 hour and 20 minutes. Let cool in pan for 10 minutes. Remove from pan and let cool completely on a wire rack. Drizzle Sugar Glaze over cake.

Spice Blend: In a small bowl, stir together all ingredients until completely combined.

Sugar Glaze: In a medium bowl, whisk together confectioners' sugar, milk, and corn syrup.

Gingerbread Bundt Cake

MAKES ABOUT 12 SERVINGS

Cake
- 1 cup unsalted butter, softened
- 1½ cups firmly packed brown sugar
- ½ cup granulated sugar
- 3 large eggs
- 3¾ cups all-purpose flour
- 2½ tablespoons ground ginger
- 2 teaspoons baking powder
- 2 teaspoons baking soda
- 1 teaspoon ground cinnamon
- ¾ teaspoon salt
- ¼ teaspoon ground cloves
- 1¾ cups whole buttermilk
- ½ cup dark unsulphured molasses
- ½ teaspoon lemon zest
- Lemon Glaze (recipe follows)
- Garnish: pomegranate seeds, fresh mint

Lemon Glaze
Makes about 1 cup
- 2 cups confectioners' sugar
- 2 tablespoons whole buttermilk
- 1 teaspoon lemon zest
- ¼ teaspoon fresh lemon juice

Preheat oven to 325°. Spray a 15-cup Bundt pan with baking spray with flour.

Cake: In large bowl, beat butter and sugars with a mixer at medium speed until fluffy, 3 to 4 minutes, stopping to scrape sides of bowl. Add eggs, one at a time, beating well after each addition.

In a large bowl, whisk together flour, ginger, baking powder, baking soda, cinnamon, salt, and cloves. In a small bowl, stir together buttermilk, molasses, and zest.

Reduce mixer speed to low. Gradually add flour mixture to butter mixture alternately with buttermilk mixture, beginning and ending with flour mixture, beating just until combined after each addition. Spoon batter into prepared pan.

Bake until a wooden pick in serted near center comes out clean, 45 to 50 minutes. Let cool in pan for 10 minutes. Remove from pan, and let cool completely on a wire rack. Drizzle with Lemon Glaze. Garnish with pomegranate seeds and mint, if desired.

Lemon Glaze: In a medium bowl, whisk together all ingredients until smooth.

Double Chocolate-Spice Bundt Cake

MAKES ABOUT 12 SERVINGS

Cake
- 1 cup whole milk
- 2 chai tea bags
- 1 cup unsalted butter, softened
- 1½ cups firmly packed brown sugar
- 3 large eggs
- 3 cups all-purpose flour
- ¾ teaspoon baking powder
- ½ teaspoon baking soda
- ½ teaspoon salt
- 1 cup whole buttermilk
- 1 teaspoon vanilla extract
- 2 (4-ounce) bars bittersweet chocolate, finely chopped
- 1 cup semisweet chocolate morsels, melted and slightly cooled

Chai Milk Glaze (recipe follows)

Chai Milk Glaze
- 3 ounces bittersweet chocolate, melted
- 1½ cups confectioners' sugar
- 1 tablespoon unsalted butter
- 5 tablespoons reserved chai milk

Preheat oven to 300°. Spray a 10- to 15-cup Bundt pan with baking spray with flour.

Cake: In a small saucepan, bring milk to a simmer over medium heat. Remove from heat. Add tea bags; cover and let stand for 10 minutes. Discard tea bags. Reserve ½ cup chai milk for batter and 5 tablespoons chai milk for Chai Milk Glaze.

In a large bowl, beat butter and brown sugar with a mixer at medium speed until fluffy, 3 to 4 minutes, stopping to scrape sides of bowl. Add eggs, one at a time, beating well after each addition.

In a medium bowl, whisk together flour, baking powder, baking soda, and salt. In a small bowl, whisk together buttermilk, reserved ½ cup chai milk, and vanilla.

Reduce mixer speed to low. Gradually add flour mixture to butter mixture alternately with buttermilk mixture, beginning and ending with flour mixture, beating just until combined after each addition. Add chopped chocolate and melted chocolate, beating just until combined. Spoon batter into prepared pan. Tap pan twice on counter to release any air bubbles.

Bake until a wooden pick inserted near center comes out clean, about 1 hour and 10 minutes. Let cool in pan for 10 minutes. Remove from pan, and let cool completely on a wire rack. Drizzle Chai Milk Glaze over cake.

Chai Milk Glaze: In a medium bowl, whisk together melted chocolate, confectioners' sugar, butter, and reserved chai milk, adding 1 tablespoon at a time, until desired consistency is reached.

Rich chocolate and chai spices make this cake perfect for any chocolate lover.

Ginger Pound Cake with Maple Glaze

MAKES ABOUT 12 SERVINGS

Cake
- ½ cup unsalted butter, softened
- ½ cup all-vegetable shortening
- 2 cups sugar
- 5 large eggs
- 1½ teaspoons vanilla extract
- 2 cups all-purpose flour
- 1 tablespoon ground ginger
- ¼ teaspoon salt
- ½ cup whole milk
- Maple Glaze (recipe follows)
- Garnish: chopped candied ginger, chopped pecans

Maple Glaze
- ½ cup confectioners' sugar
- 3 to 4 tablespoons maple syrup
- 1 teaspoon maple flavoring

Preheat oven to 300°. Spray a 10- to 15-cup Bundt pan with baking spray with flour.

Cake: In large bowl, beat butter, shortening, and sugar with a mixer at medium speed until fluffy, 3 to 4 minutes, stopping to scrape sides of bowl. Add eggs, one at a time, beating well after each addition. Beat in vanilla.

In medium bowl, sift together flour, ginger, and salt. Reduce mixer speed to low. Gradually add flour mixture to butter mixture alternately with milk, beginning and ending with flour mixture, beating just until combined after each addition. Spoon batter into prepared pan.

Bake until a wooden pick inserted near center comes out clean, 1 hour and 10 minutes to 1 hour and 15 minutes, loosely covering with foil during last 20 minutes of baking to prevent excess browning. Let cool in pan for 10 minutes. Remove from pan, and let cool completely on a wire rack. Drizzle Maple Glaze over cake. Garnish with candied ginger and pecans, if desired.

Maple Glaze: In small bowl, combine confectioners' sugar, 3 tablespoons maple syrup, and maple flavoring. Add remaining 1 tablespoon maple syrup if a thinner consistency is desired.

Chocolate-Coconut Bundt Cake

MAKES ABOUT 12 SERVINGS

Cake
1 cup unsalted butter
1½ cups sugar
3 large eggs
1 teaspoon vanilla extract
2 cups all-purpose flour
¼ cup unsweetened cocoa powder
1 teaspoon baking soda
¾ teaspoon salt
½ teaspoon baking powder
1 cup water
Coconut Filling (recipe follows)
Coconut Milk Glaze (recipe follows)

Coconut Filing
1 cup sweetened flaked coconut
2 tablespoons sugar
2 tablespoons all-purpose flour
½ teaspoon vanilla extract
⅛ teaspoon salt
1 large egg white
½ cup dark chocolate morsels

Coconut Milk Glaze
1½ cups confectioners' sugar
3 to 4 tablespoons coconut milk

Preheat oven to 350°. Spray a 15-cup Bundt pan with baking spray with flour.

Cake: In a large bowl, beat butter and sugar with a mixer at medium speed until fluffy, 3 to 4 minutes, stopping to scrape sides of bowl. Add eggs, one at a time, beating well after each addition. Beat in vanilla.

In a medium bowl, whisk together flour, cocoa, baking soda, salt, and baking powder. Reduce mixer speed to low. Gradually add flour mixture to butter mixture alternately with 1 cup water, beginning and ending with flour mixture, beating just until combined after each addition.

Spoon half of batter into prepared pan. Spoon Coconut Filling over batter, avoiding edges of pan. Spoon remaining batter over filling. Smooth top with an offset spatula.

Bake until a wooden pick inserted near center comes out clean, about 45 minutes. Let cool in pan for 15 minutes. Remove from pan, and let cool completely on a wire rack. Spoon Coconut Milk Glaze over cake. Let stand until glaze is set, about 30 minutes.

Coconut Filling: In a medium bowl, combine coconut, sugar, flour, vanilla, salt, and egg white. Stir in chocolate.

Coconut Milk Glaze: In a medium bowl, place confectioners' sugar. Whisk in coconut milk, 1 tablespoon at a time, until glaze reaches a thick consistency.

German Chocolate Pound Cake

MAKES ABOUT 16 SERVINGS

Cake
- 1 cup unsalted butter, softened
- 2 cups sugar
- 4 large eggs
- 1 cup sour cream
- 1 teaspoon vanilla extract
- 2 cups all-purpose flour
- 2 tablespoons natural unsweetened cocoa powder
- ½ teaspoon baking soda
- ½ teaspoon salt
- 1 (4-ounce) bar German's sweet chocolate, melted and cooled

Coconut-Pecan Frosting (recipe follows)

Coconut-Pecan Frosting
Makes about 2 cups
- 1 (5-ounce) can evaporated milk
- ¾ cup sugar
- ⅓ cup butter
- 2 egg yolks
- 1½ cups sweetened flaked coconut
- ¾ cup chopped pecans

Preheat oven to 325°. Spray a 10- to 15-cup Bundt pan with baking spray with flour.

Cake: In a large bowl, beat butter and sugar with a mixer at medium speed until fluffy, 3 to 4 minutes, stopping to scrape sides of bowl. Add eggs, one at a time, beating well after each addition. Beat in sour cream and vanilla.

In a medium bowl, whisk together flour, cocoa, baking soda, and salt. Reduce mixer speed to low. Gradually add flour mixture to butter mixture, beating just until combined. Add melted chocolate, beating until combined. Spoon batter into prepared pan.

Bake until a wooden pick inserted near center comes out clean, about 1 hour. Let cool in pan for 10 minutes. Remove from pan, and let cool completely on a wire rack. Spoon Coconut-Pecan Frosting on top of cooled cake.

Coconut-Pecan Frosting: In a medium saucepan, combine evaporated milk, sugar, butter, and egg yolks. Cook over medium heat, stirring constantly, until thickened and golden brown, about 15 minutes. Remove from heat; stir in coconut and pecans.

Caramel Apple Pound Cake

MAKES ABOUT 16 SERVINGS

Cake
1 cup granulated sugar
1¼ cups firmly packed brown sugar, divided
1½ cups unsalted butter, melted
4 large eggs
1 teaspoon vanilla extract
3 cups all-purpose flour
2 teaspoons baking powder
1 teaspoon salt
1 teaspoon apple pie spice
3 cups chopped Granny Smith apple
2 teaspoons ground cinnamon
Cream Cheese Icing (recipe follows)
Garnish: chopped walnuts, hot caramel topping*

Cream Cheese Icing
Makes about 2 cups
1 (8-ounce) package cream cheese, softened
2 cups confectioners' sugar
¼ cup whole milk
¼ cup hot caramel topping*

Preheat oven to 350°. Spray a 12-cup Bundt pan with baking spray with flour.

Cake: In a large bowl, beat granulated sugar, 1 cup brown sugar, and melted butter with a mixer at medium speed until fluffy, 3 to 4 minutes, stopping to scrape sides of bowl. Add eggs, one at a time, beating well after each addition. Beat in vanilla.

In a medium bowl, whisk together flour, baking powder, salt, and apple pie spice. Reduce mixer speed to low. Gradually add flour mixture to butter mixture, beating just until combined.

In another medium bowl, combine apple, cinnamon, and remaining ¼ cup brown sugar.

Spoon one-third of batter into prepared pan; top with half of apple mixture. Repeat layers once. Top with remaining one-third of batter.

Bake until a wooden pick inserted near center comes out clean, 50 minutes to 1 hour. Let cool in pan for 10 minutes. Remove from pan, and let cool completely on a wire rack. Top with Cream Cheese Icing. Garnish with walnuts and caramel topping, if desired.

Cream Cheese Icing: In a medium bowl, beat cream cheese and confectioners' sugar with a mixer at medium-low speed until smooth. Beat in milk and caramel topping.

**We used Smucker's Hot Caramel Topping.*

Chocolate Bundt Cake with Baileys Custard Glaze

MAKES ABOUT 14 SERVINGS

Cake
1 cup unsalted butter, softened
1½ cups sugar
4 large eggs
1 teaspoon vanilla extract
2½ cups all-purpose flour
½ cup unsweetened cocoa powder
1 teaspoon baking soda
¾ teaspoon salt
1 cup whole buttermilk
Baileys Custard Glaze (recipe follows)
Garnish: grated chocolate

Baileys Custard Glaze
Makes about 1 cup
1 cup Irish cream liqueur*
2 large eggs
¼ cup sugar
2 tablespoons unsalted butter
1 teaspoon vanilla extract

Preheat oven to 325°. Spray a 15-cup Bundt pan with baking spray with flour.

Cake: In a large bowl, beat butter and sugar with a mixer at medium speed until fluffy, 3 to 4 minutes, stopping to scrape sides of bowl. Add eggs, one at a time, beating well after each addition. Beat in vanilla.

In a medium bowl, whisk together flour, cocoa, baking soda, and salt. Reduce mixer speed to low. Gradually add flour mixture to butter mixture alternately with buttermilk, beginning and ending with flour mixture, beating just until combined after each addition. Spoon batter into prepared pan.

Bake until a wooden pick inserted near center comes out clean, about 1 hour. Let cool completely in pan. Remove from pan. Drizzle with Baileys Custard Glaze. Garnish with grated chocolate, if desired.

Baileys Custard Glaze: In a small saucepan, heat liqueur over medium heat until simmering.

In a medium bowl, whisk together eggs and sugar. Add hot liqueur, ½ cup at a time, whisking rapidly and constantly until well combined. Return mixture to saucepan; cook, stirring constantly, until thickened, about 1 minute. Pour into a clean bowl; whisk in butter and vanilla. Let cool. Refrigerate until ready to use.

**We used Baileys Original Irish Cream.*

Red Velvet Pound Cake

MAKES ABOUT 14 SERVINGS

Cake

- 1½ cups unsalted butter, softened
- 3 cups sugar
- 5 large eggs
- 3 cups all-purpose flour
- ⅓ cup unsweetened cocoa powder
- ½ teaspoon salt
- ¼ teaspoon baking soda
- 1 cup whole buttermilk
- 1 (1-ounce) bottle liquid red food coloring
- 1 teaspoon distilled white vinegar
- 1 teaspoon vanilla extract

Cream Cheese Glaze (recipe follows)

Cream Cheese Glaze
Makes about ¾ cup

- 1 (3-ounce) package cream cheese, softened
- 1½ cups confectioners' sugar
- 1 tablespoon milk

Preheat oven to 350°. Spray a 12-cup Bundt pan with baking spray with flour.

Cake: In a large bowl, beat butter and sugar with a mixer at medium speed until fluffy, 3 to 4 minutes, stopping to scrape sides of bowl. Add eggs, one at a time, beating well after each addition.

In a medium bowl, combine flour, cocoa, salt, and baking soda. In a small bowl, combine buttermilk, food coloring, vinegar, and vanilla. Reduce mixer speed to low. Gradually add flour mixture to butter mixture alternately with buttermilk mixture, beating just until combined after each addition. Spoon batter into prepared pan.

Bake until a wooden pick inserted near center comes out clean, 50 minutes to 1 hour. Let cool in pan for 10 minutes. Remove from pan, and let cool completely on a wire rack. Drizzle cooled cake with Cream Cheese Glaze.

Cream Cheese Glaze: In a small bowl, beat cream cheese with a mixer at low speed until creamy. Gradually add confectioners' sugar, beating until combined. Add milk, beating until smooth.

Chocolate Bundt Cake

MAKES ABOUT 14 SERVINGS

- 1½ cups unsalted butter, softened
- 2½ cups sugar
- 4 large eggs
- 2 teaspoons vanilla extract
- 2¾ cups all-purpose flour
- ½ cup unsweetened cocoa powder
- 1½ teaspoons salt
- 1 teaspoon baking powder
- 1 teaspoon baking soda
- 1 cup hot coffee
- 2 (4-ounce) bars bittersweet chocolate, chopped
- 1 cup whole buttermilk
- 1 (12.25-ounce) jar caramel sauce,* unheated
- ⅓ cup chopped toasted pecans

Preheat oven to 325°. Spray a 15-cup Bundt pan with baking spray with flour.

In a large bowl, beat butter and sugar with a mixer at medium speed until fluffy, 3 to 4 minutes, stopping to scrape sides of bowl. Add eggs, one at a time, beating well after each addition. Beat in vanilla.

In a medium bowl, whisk together flour, cocoa, salt, baking powder, and baking soda. In a small bowl, stir together hot coffee and chocolate until melted; stir in buttermilk.

Reduce mixer speed to low. Gradually add flour mixture to butter mixture alternately with chocolate mixture, beginning and ending with flour mixture, beating just until combined after each addition. Spoon batter into prepared pan.

Bake until a wooden pick inserted near center comes out clean, about 1 hour and 5 minutes. Let cool in pan for 10 minutes. Remove from pan, and let cool completely on a wire rack. Drizzle with caramel sauce, and top with pecans.

**We used Smucker's Hot Caramel Topping.*

German Chocolate Bundt Cake with Butterscotch Glaze

MAKES ABOUT 10 SERVINGS

Cake
- ¾ cup unsweetened cocoa powder
- ¾ (4-ounce) bar German's sweet chocolate, chopped
- ¾ cup hot coffee
- ½ cup unsalted butter, softened
- 2 cups sugar
- 3 teaspoons vanilla extract
- 3 egg whites, room temperature
- 3 cups all-purpose flour
- 3 teaspoons baking powder
- 1½ teaspoons salt
- ¾ teaspoon baking soda
- 1½ cups whole buttermilk
- Butterscotch Glaze (recipe follows)

Butterscotch Glaze
Makes about 1 cup
- 1 cup butterscotch morsels
- ½ cup half-and-half

Preheat oven to 350°. Spray a 10-cup Bundt pan with baking spray with flour.

Cake: In a medium bowl, whisk together cocoa, chocolate, and hot coffee. Set aside.

In a large bowl, beat butter, sugar, and vanilla with a mixer at medium speed until fluffy, 3 to 4 minutes, stopping to scrape sides of bowl. Add egg whites, one at a time, beating well after each addition. Reduce mixer speed to low, and add chocolate mixture, beating until combined.

In another medium bowl, whisk together flour, baking powder, salt, and baking soda. Gradually add flour mixture to butter mixture alternately with buttermilk, beginning and ending with flour mixture, beating just until combined after each addition. Spoon batter into prepared pan.

Bake until a wooden pick inserted near center comes out clean, about 1 hour. Let cool in pan for 10 minutes. Remove from pan, and let cool completely on a wire rack. Pour Butterscotch Glaze over cake. Store at room temperature for up to 5 days.

Butterscotch Glaze: In a small saucepan, combine butterscotch morsels and half-and-half. Cook over medium heat, whisking frequently, until mixture is smooth and morsels are melted. Let cool until thickened, about 15 minutes. Use immediately. If glaze becomes firm, place in a microwavable bowl, and microwave on high until melted and smooth, 10 to 15 seconds.

Lemon Poppy Seed Cornmeal Cake,
page 187

cake tip
We have found that spraying a pan
with baking spray with flour makes
it much easier to get a cake out of
the pan than the traditional way
of greasing and flouring. Also, it
doesn't leave your cake with a
flour taste on the outside.

Chocolate Pound Cake with Tasty Hot Fudge Sauce

MAKES ABOUT 10 SERVINGS

Cake
- 1½ cups unsalted butter, softened
- 3 cups granulated sugar
- 5 large eggs
- 1 teaspoon vanilla extract
- 3 cups all-purpose flour
- 5 tablespoons special dark cocoa powder*
- ½ teaspoon baking soda
- ½ teaspoon baking powder
- ½ teaspoon salt
- ¾ cup whole buttermilk
- ½ cup sour cream

Tasty Hot Fudge Sauce (recipe follows), to serve
Garnish: confectioners' sugar

Tasty Hot Fudge Sauce
Makes about 2½ cups
- ¾ (4-ounce) bar unsweetened chocolate, chopped
- ½ cup unsalted butter
- 1 cup granulated sugar
- ½ cup firmly packed brown sugar
- 1 cup heavy whipping cream
- 1 teaspoon vanilla extract

Preheat oven to 325°. Spray a 12- to 15-cup Bundt pan with baking spray with flour.

Cake: In a large bowl, beat butter and granulated sugar with a mixer at medium speed until fluffy, 3 to 4 minutes, stopping to scrape sides of bowl. Add eggs, one at a time, beating well after each addition. Beat in vanilla.

In a medium bowl, whisk together flour, cocoa, baking soda, baking powder, and salt. Reduce mixer speed to low. Gradually add flour mixture to butter mixture alternately with buttermilk, beginning and ending with flour mixture, beating just until combined after each addition. Stir in sour cream. Spoon batter into prepared pan.

Bake until a wooden pick inserted near center comes out clean, about 1 hour. Let cool in pan for 10 minutes. Remove from pan, and let cool completely on a wire rack. Serve with Tasty Hot Fudge Sauce. Garnish with confectioners' sugar, if desired.

Tasty Hot Fudge Sauce: In a medium saucepan, heat chocolate and butter over medium heat. Cook, stirring frequently, until chocolate is melted and mixture is smooth. Stir in sugars. Add cream; bring to a boil over medium-high heat. Reduce heat, and simmer for 5 minutes, stirring frequently. Remove from heat, and stir in vanilla. Cover and refrigerate for up to 1 week.

**We used Hershey's Special Dark Cocoa Powder.*

Cream Cheese-Filled Red Velvet Pound Cake

MAKES ABOUT 12 SERVINGS

Cake
- 1½ cups unsalted butter, softened
- 3 cups granulated sugar
- 5 large eggs
- 1 teaspoon distilled white vinegar
- 1 teaspoon vanilla extract
- 3 cups all-purpose flour
- ⅓ cup unsweetened cocoa powder
- ½ teaspoon salt
- ¼ teaspoon baking soda
- 1 cup whole buttermilk
- 1 (1-ounce) bottle liquid red food coloring
- Cream Cheese Filling (recipe follows)
- 1 cup confectioners' sugar
- 2 tablespoons heavy whipping cream

Cream Cheese Filling
Makes about 1 cup
- 1 (8-ounce) package cream cheese, softened
- ⅓ cup granulated sugar
- 1 large egg
- 1 teaspoon vanilla extract

Preheat oven to 325°. Spray a 12- to 15-cup Bundt pan with baking spray with flour.

Cake: In a large bowl, beat butter and granulated sugar with a mixer at medium speed until fluffy, 3 to 4 minutes, stopping to scrape sides of bowl. Add eggs, one at a time, beating well after each addition. Beat in vinegar and vanilla.

In a medium bowl, combine flour, cocoa, salt, and baking soda. Reduce mixer speed to low. Gradually add flour mixture to butter mixture alternately with buttermilk, beginning and ending with flour mixture, beating just until combined after each addition. Stir in food coloring. Spoon half of batter into prepared pan. Top with Cream Cheese Filling. Spoon remaining batter over filling.

Bake until a wooden pick inserted near center comes out clean, 1 hour and 10 minutes to 1 hour and 15 minutes. Let cool in pan for 10 minutes. Remove from pan, and let cool completely on a wire rack.

In a small bowl, whisk together confectioners' sugar and cream until smooth. Drizzle over cooled cake, and sprinkle with cake crumbles, if desired. Cover and refrigerate for up to 3 days.

Cream Cheese Filling: In a small bowl, beat cream cheese and sugar with a mixer at medium speed until smooth. Add egg and vanilla, beating until combined.

Chocolate Pound Cake

MAKES ABOUT 12 SERVINGS

Cake
- 1 (4-ounce) bar semisweet chocolate, chopped
- 1 (4-ounce) bar bittersweet chocolate, chopped
- 1 cup unsalted butter, softened
- 1½ cups sugar
- 4 large eggs
- ½ cup dark corn syrup
- 1 tablespoon vanilla extract
- 2¼ cups all-purpose flour
- ¼ cup unsweetened cocoa powder
- ½ teaspoon salt
- ¼ teaspoon baking soda
- 1 cup whole buttermilk
- Buttermilk Glaze (recipe follows)
- Garnish: sugared cranberries, sugared rosemary

Buttermilk Glaze
Makes about 2 cups
- 2 cups confectioners' sugar
- ½ cup whole buttermilk
- 1 teaspoon vanilla extract

Preheat oven to 325°. Spray a 15-cup Bundt pan with baking spray with flour.

Cake: In a medium microwave-safe bowl, heat chocolates on high in 30-second intervals, stirring between each, until melted and smooth (about 1½ minutes total).

In a large bowl, beat butter and sugar with a mixer at medium speed until fluffy, 3 to 4 minutes, stopping to scrape sides of bowl. Add eggs, one at a time, beating well after each addition. Add corn syrup, vanilla, and melted chocolate, beating to combine.

In a medium bowl, whisk together flour, cocoa, salt, and baking soda. Reduce mixer speed to low. Gradually add flour mixture to butter mixture alternately with buttermilk, beginning and ending with flour mixture, beating just until combined after each addition. Spoon batter into prepared pan.

Bake until a wooden pick inserted near center comes out clean, about 1 hour and 10 minutes. Let cool in pan for 10 minutes. Remove from pan, and let cool completely on a wire rack. Pour Buttermilk Glaze over cooled cake. Garnish with sugared cranberries and sugared rosemary, if desired.

Buttermilk Glaze: In a small bowl, whisk together confectioners' sugar and buttermilk until smooth. Add vanilla, and stir to combine. Use immediately.

Vanilla Pound Cake with Peppermint Glaze

MAKES ABOUT 12 SERVINGS

Cake
1 cup unsalted butter, softened
½ cup butter-flavored shortening
3 cups sugar
5 large eggs
½ vanilla bean, split lengthwise, seeds scraped and reserved
3 cups all-purpose flour
1 tablespoon vanilla powder*
1 teaspoon salt
½ teaspoon baking powder
1 cup whole buttermilk
2 teaspoons vanilla extract
Peppermint Glaze (recipe follows)
Garnish: crushed peppermints

Peppermint Glaze
Makes about 1½ cups
1½ cups confectioners' sugar
3 tablespoons whole milk
½ teaspoon peppermint extract

Preheat oven to 325°. Spray a 15-cup Bundt pan with baking spray with flour.

Cake: In a large bowl, beat butter, shortening, and sugar with a mixer at medium speed until fluffy, 3 to 4 minutes, stopping to scrape sides of bowl. Add eggs, one at a time, beating well after each addition. Beat in reserved vanilla bean seeds.

In a medium bowl, sift together flour, vanilla powder, salt, and baking powder. In a small bowl, stir together buttermilk and vanilla extract. Reduce mixer speed to low. Gradually add flour mixture to butter mixture alternately with buttermilk mixture, beginning and ending with flour mixture, beating just until combined after each addition. Spoon batter into prepared pan. Tap pan on counter to release any air bubbles.

Bake for 45 minutes. Cover with foil, and bake until a wooden pick inserted near center comes out clean, about 45 minutes more. Let cool in pan for 20 minutes. Remove from pan, and let cool completely on a wire rack. Pour Peppermint Glaze over cooled cake. Garnish with crushed peppermints, if desired.

Peppermint Glaze: In a small bowl, whisk together confectioners' sugar, milk, and peppermint extract until smooth. Use immediately.

**We used Nielsen-Massey Madagascar Bourbon Pure Vanilla Powder, which can be purchased at specialty foods stores or online.*

Candied Apple-Pear Bundt Cake

MAKES ABOUT 12 SERVINGS

Cake
- 3 cups sugar, divided
- ½ cup cane syrup*
- 1½ cups plus 2 tablespoons unsalted butter, softened and divided
- 2 large Granny Smith apples, peeled, cored, and sliced
- 2 Bosc pears, peeled, cored, and sliced
- 5 large eggs
- 2 teaspoons vanilla extract
- 3 cups all-purpose flour
- 2 teaspoons ground cinnamon
- 1 teaspoon grated fresh nutmeg
- 1 teaspoon salt
- ½ teaspoon baking soda
- 1 cup sour cream
- Cane Syrup Glaze (recipe follows)

Cane Syrup Glaze
Makes about 1 cup
- ⅔ cup reserved fruit syrup
- 2 cups confectioners' sugar
- 2 tablespoons whole buttermilk

Preheat oven to 325°. Spray a 15-cup Bundt pan with baking spray with flour.

Cake: In a large skillet, bring 1 cup sugar and cane syrup to a boil over medium-high heat. Cook, stirring constantly, until sugar dissolves, about 2 minutes. Stir in 2 tablespoons butter until melted. Add apple and pear, stirring to combine. Reduce heat to medium; cook, stirring occasionally, until fruit softens, about 12 minutes. Remove from heat, and let cool completely.

In a large bowl, beat remaining 1½ cups butter and remaining 2 cups sugar with a mixer at medium speed until fluffy, 3 to 4 minutes, stopping to scrape sides of bowl. Add eggs, one at a time, beating well after each addition. Beat in vanilla.

In a medium bowl, stir together flour, cinnamon, nutmeg, salt, and baking soda. Reduce mixer speed to low. Gradually add flour mixture to butter mixture alternately with sour cream, beginning and ending with flour mixture, beating just until combined after each addition.

Reserve ⅔ cup syrup from fruit mixture for Cane Syrup Glaze. Gently fold remaining syrup and fruit mixture into batter. Spoon batter into prepared pan.

Bake until a wooden pick inserted near center comes out clean, about 1 hour and 10 minutes. Let cool in pan for 10 minutes. Remove from pan, and let cool completely on a wire rack. Drizzle with Cane Syrup Glaze.

Cane Syrup Glaze: In a small bowl, stir together reserved ⅔ cup syrup, confectioners' sugar, and buttermilk until smooth.

**We used Steen's Pure Cane Syrup.*

Kentucky Browned Butter Bundt Cake

MAKES ABOUT 10 SERVINGS

Cake
- 1 cup unsalted butter, softened
- 2 cups sugar
- 4 large eggs
- 3 cups all-purpose flour
- 1½ teaspoons salt
- 1 teaspoon baking powder
- ½ teaspoon baking soda
- ½ teaspoon ground nutmeg
- ½ teaspoon ground cloves
- ¼ teaspoon ground cardamom
- 1 cup whole buttermilk
- 3 teaspoons vanilla extract
- Browned Butter Glaze (recipe follows)
- Fresh cranberries, to serve

Browned Butter Glaze
Makes about ½ cup
- 2 tablespoons butter
- 1 tablespoon water
- 6 tablespoons sugar
- 1 teaspoon vanilla extract

Preheat oven to 325°. Spray a 10-cup Bundt pan with baking spray with flour.

Cake: In a large bowl, beat butter and sugar with a mixer at medium speed until fluffy, 3 to 4 minutes, stopping to scrape sides of bowl. Add eggs, one at a time, beating just until combined after each addition.

In another large bowl, whisk together flour, salt, baking powder, baking soda, nutmeg, cloves, and cardamom. In a small bowl, stir together buttermilk and vanilla.

Reduce mixer speed to low. Gradually add flour mixture to butter mixture alternately with buttermilk mixture, beginning and ending with flour mixture, beating just until combined after each addition. Spoon batter into prepared pan.

Bake until a wooden pick inserted near center comes out clean, 1 hour to 1 hour and 5 minutes. Let cool in pan for 15 minutes. Remove from pan. Pour Browned Butter Glaze over warm cake. Let cool completely until sugar has crystallized, about 1 hour. Serve with cranberries.

Browned Butter Glaze: In a small saucepan, melt butter over medium-low heat. Cook until butter is light brown, about 12 minutes. Add 1 tablespoon water, sugar, and vanilla; bring to a simmer. Cook, stirring frequently, until sugar is dissolved, about 1 minute.

Chocolate Carrot Cake

MAKES ABOUT 14 SERVINGS

Cake
1 cup granulated sugar
1 cup firmly packed dark brown sugar
1 cup vegetable oil
4 large eggs
1 tablespoon vanilla extract
2 cups all-purpose flour
1 tablespoon ground cinnamon
2 teaspoons baking powder
¾ teaspoon salt
1 teaspoon ground ginger
½ teaspoon baking soda
½ teaspoon ground nutmeg
3 cups shredded carrots
¾ cup chopped semisweet chocolate
Cream Cheese Glaze (recipe follows)
Garnish: chopped semisweet chocolate

Cream Cheese Glaze
1 (8-ounce) package cream cheese, softened
2 tablespoons confectioners' sugar
2 tablespoons whole milk
⅛ teaspoon salt

Preheat oven to 350°. Spray a 13-cup cast-iron fluted cake pan with baking spray with flour.

Cake: In a large bowl, whisk together sugars, oil, eggs, and vanilla until well combined.

In a medium bowl, whisk together flour, cinnamon, baking powder, salt, ginger, baking soda, and nutmeg. Gradually add flour mixture to sugar mixture, whisking until just combined. Fold in carrots and chocolate.

Spoon batter into prepared pan. Gently tap pan on counter lined with a kitchen towel a few times to release air bubbles.

Bake until a wooden pick inserted near center comes out clean, 45 to 50 minutes. Let cool in pan on a wire rack for 15 minutes. Remove cake onto wire rack, and let cool completely. Top with Cream Cheese Glaze. Refrigerate until ready to serve. Garnish with chopped chocolate, if desired.

Cream Cheese Glaze: In a medium bowl, beat cream cheese with mixer on medium speed until smooth. Add confectioners' sugar, milk, and salt, beating until well combined and smooth.

Churro and Chocolate Pound Cake

MAKES ABOUT 12 SERVINGS

- 1½ cups unsalted butter, softened
- 2 cups plus 2 tablespoons firmly packed brown sugar, divided
- 5 large eggs
- 2 teaspoons vanilla extract
- 3 cups all-purpose flour
- 2 teaspoons ground cinnamon, divided
- 1 teaspoon kosher salt
- 1 teaspoon baking powder
- ½ teaspoon ground nutmeg
- 1 cup sour cream
- ½ cup whole milk
- ¼ cup granulated sugar
- 2 tablespoons melted unsalted butter
- Chocolate sauce, to serve

Preheat oven to 350°. Spray a 13-cup cast-iron fluted cake pan with baking spray with flour.

In the bowl of a stand mixer fitted with the paddle attachment, beat butter and 2 cups brown sugar with a mixer at medium speed until fluffy, 2 to 3 minutes, stopping to scrape sides of bowl. Add eggs, one at a time, beating well after each addition. Beat in vanilla.

In a large bowl, whisk together flour, 1 teaspoon cinnamon, salt, baking powder, and nutmeg. In a medium bowl, whisk together sour cream and milk. With mixer at low speed, gradually add flour mixture to butter mixture alternately with sour cream mixture, beginning and ending with flour mixture, beating just until combined after each addition.

Spoon batter into prepared pan. Gently tap pan on counter lined with a kitchen towel a few times to release air bubbles.

Bake until a wooden pick inserted near center comes out clean, about 1 hour and 10 minutes. Let cool in pan on a wire rack for 15 minutes. Remove from pan onto wire rack, and let cool completely.

In a small bowl, stir together granulated sugar, remaining 2 tablespoons brown sugar, and remaining 1 teaspoon cinnamon. Working in sections, brush cake with melted butter and coat with sugar mixture, pressing gently to adhere. Serve with chocolate sauce.

Blackberry-Lemon Cornmeal Bundt

MAKES ABOUT 10 SERVINGS

Cake
- 1⅓ cups unsalted butter, melted
- ¾ cup sugar
- ½ cup clover honey
- ⅓ cup whole buttermilk, room temperature
- 4 large eggs
- 1 large egg yolk
- 4 teaspoons packed lemon zest
- 2 tablespoons fresh lemon juice
- 1⅔ cups self-rising white cornmeal mix*
- 1½ cups all-purpose flour
- 1 teaspoon kosher salt
- ½ teaspoon baking powder
- ¼ teaspoon baking soda
- ½ cup seedless blackberry preserves
- Lemon Zest Glaze (recipe follows)
- Garnish: fresh blackberries, fresh mint

Lemon Zest Glaze
- 1½ cups confectioners' sugar
- 2 teaspoons lemon zest
- 2 tablespoons plus 1 teaspoon fresh lemon juice
- 1 tablespoon unsalted butter, melted

Preheat oven to 325°. Spray a 10-cup Bundt pan with baking spray with flour.

Cake: In a large bowl, whisk together melted butter, sugar, honey, buttermilk, eggs, egg yolk, zest, and juice.

In a medium bowl, whisk together cornmeal mix, flour, salt, baking powder, and baking soda. Gradually whisk cornmeal mixture into butter mixture just until some dry streaks remain. Transfer ¼ cup batter to a small bowl, and stir in preserves.

Spoon plain batter into prepared pan. Tap pan on a towel-lined counter to release any air bubbles. Gently spoon blackberry batter in center of batter, avoiding sides of pan. Using a knife, gently swirl blackberry batter into plain batter, being careful to not touch sides of pan.

Bake until a wooden pick inserted near center comes out clean, 50 minutes to 1 hour. Let cool in pan on a wire rack for 15 minutes. Remove from pan onto wire rack, and let cool completely. Drizzle Lemon Zest Glaze onto cooled cake, and let stand until set, about 10 minutes. Store in an airtight container for up to 3 days. Garnish with blackberries and mint, if desired.

Lemon Zest Glaze: In a small bowl, whisk together all ingredients until smooth.

**We used Martha White Self-Rising Cornmeal Mix.*

Sweet Potato Pound Cake with Cane Syrup Glaze and Pecans

MAKES ABOUT 12 SERVINGS

Cake
- 1 cup Candied Pecans (recipe follows)
- ¼ cup firmly packed brown sugar
- 2 cups plus 3 tablespoons all-purpose flour, divided
- ½ teaspoon apple pie spice
- 1 cup unsalted butter, softened
- 2 cups granulated sugar
- 4 large eggs
- 1 cup mashed sweet potato, cooled
- 1 teaspoon vanilla extract
- ½ teaspoon baking soda
- ⅛ teaspoon salt
- Cane Syrup Glaze (recipe follows)
- Garnish: Candied Pecans

Cane Syrup Glaze
- ¾ cup confectioners' sugar
- 6 tablespoons heavy whipping cream
- 2 tablespoons cane syrup*

Candied Pecans
- 2 cups pecans, roughly chopped
- 1 large egg white
- ⅓ cup firmly packed dark brown sugar

Preheat oven to 325°. Spray a 10-cup Bundt pan with baking spray with flour.

Cake: In a medium bowl, whisk together Candied Pecans, brown sugar, 1 tablespoon flour, and apple pie spice. Set aside.

In the bowl of a stand mixer fitted with the paddle attachment, beat butter and granulated sugar at medium speed until fluffy, 3 to 4 minutes, stopping to scrape sides of bowl. Add eggs, one at a time, beating well after each addition. Beat in sweet potato and vanilla until smooth.

In a large bowl, whisk together baking soda, salt, and remaining 2 cups plus 2 tablespoons flour. With mixer at low speed, gradually add flour mixture to butter mixture, beating until combined. Spoon half of batter into prepared pan. Sprinkle with pecan crumble. Spoon remaining batter on top of pecan crumble, smoothing top with an offset spatula.

Bake until a wooden pick inserted near center comes out clean, about 1 hour. Let cool in pan for 20 minutes. Remove from pan, and let cool completely on a wire rack. Spoon Cane Syrup Glaze over cooled cake. Garnish with Candied Pecans, if desired.

Cane Syrup Glaze: In a medium bowl, whisk together confectioners' sugar, cream, and cane syrup until smooth.

Candied Pecans: Preheat oven to 350°. Line a rimmed baking sheet with a nonstick silicone baking mat or parchment paper.

In a large bowl, stir together all ingredients until combined. Transfer to prepared pan, spreading in an even layer.

Bake until toasted, about 8 minutes. Let cool on a wire rack.

**We used Steen's Pure Cane Syrup.*

Lemon Poppy Seed Cornmeal Cake

MAKES ABOUT 10 SERVINGS

Cake

- 1 cup unsalted butter, softened
- 1½ cups sugar
- 3 large eggs
- 1 tablespoon lemon zest
- 1 tablespoon fresh lemon juice
- 1 teaspoon vanilla extract
- 1 cup all-purpose flour
- 1 cup finely ground plain yellow cornmeal
- 1 tablespoon poppy seeds
- 1 teaspoon baking powder
- ⅛ teaspoon salt
- ⅓ cup whole buttermilk

Boiled Lemon Sugar Glaze

- 1 cup confectioners' sugar
- 2 tablespoons lemon zest
- ½ cup fresh lemon juice
- ⅛ teaspoon salt

Preheat oven to 325°. Spray a 6-cup cast-iron fluted cake pan with cooking spray with flour.

Cake: In a large bowl, beat butter and sugar with a mixer at medium speed until fluffy, 3 to 4 minutes. Add eggs, one at a time, beating well after each addition. Beat in zest, juice, and vanilla.

In a medium bowl, whisk together flour, cornmeal, poppy seeds, baking powder, and salt. With mixer at low speed, gradually add flour mixture to butter mixture alternately with buttermilk, beginning and ending with flour mixture, beating just until combined after each addition.

Spoon batter into prepared pan. Gently tap pan on counter lined with a kitchen towel a few times to release air bubbles.

Bake until a wooden pick inserted near center comes out clean, about 45 minutes. Let cool in pan on a wire rack for 10 minutes. Remove from pan onto wire rack, and let cool completely. Spoon hot Boiled Lemon Sugar Glaze on top and sides of cake.

Boiled Lemon Sugar Glaze: In a small saucepan, whisk together confectioners' sugar, lemon zest and juice, and salt over medium heat. Bring to a boil, stirring frequently, until sugar dissolves and thickens slightly, about 2 minutes. Use immediately.

loaves & mini cakes

Versatile loaf and mini loaf pans, as well as baking cups and skillets, are useful for pound cake loaves and mini cakes. Individual servings can be created in a snap!

Chocolate-Vanilla Swirl Pound Cake, page 203

Buttermilk Pound Cake

MAKES 1 (9X5-INCH) LOAF

Cake
- ¾ cup unsalted butter, softened
- 1½ cups sugar
- 3 large eggs, room temperature
- 1½ cups all-purpose flour, sifted
- ½ teaspoon salt
- ½ cup whole buttermilk
- Buttermilk Whipped Cream (recipe follows)

Buttermilk Whipped Cream
Makes about 4 cups
- 1½ cups heavy whipping cream
- ¾ cup whole buttermilk
- ½ cup confectioners' sugar

Spray a 9x5-inch loaf pan with baking spray with flour. Line pan with parchment paper, and spray pan again.

Cake: In a large bowl, beat butter and sugar with a mixer at medium speed until fluffy, 3 to 4 minutes, stopping to scrape sides of bowl. Add eggs, one at a time, beating well after each addition.

In a medium bowl, whisk together flour and salt. Reduce mixer speed to low. Gradually add flour mixture to butter mixture alternately with buttermilk, beginning and ending with flour mixture, beating just until combined after each addition. Spoon batter into prepared pan.

Place pan in a cold oven. Bake at 300° until a wooden pick inserted in center comes out clean, about 1 hour and 20 minutes. Let cool in pan for 10 minutes. Remove from pan, and let cool completely on a wire rack. Serve with Buttermilk Whipped Cream.

Buttermilk Whipped Cream: In a large bowl, beat cream, buttermilk, and confectioners' sugar with a mixer at high speed until soft peaks form, about 2 minutes. Serve immediately.

Browned Butter-Cinnamon Marble Pound Cakes with Buttermilk Glaze

MAKES 2 (9X5-INCH) LOAVES

Cakes
1 cup Browned Butter (recipe follows), room temperature
2¼ cups sugar, divided
4 large eggs
3 cups all-purpose flour
1 tablespoon baking powder
3 tablespoons ground cinnamon, divided
1½ teaspoons salt, divided
1¼ cups whole buttermilk
2 tablespoons vanilla extract
Buttermilk Glaze (recipe follows)
Garnish: chopped pecans

Browned Butter
Makes 1 cup
1¼ cups unsalted butter

Buttermilk Glaze
Makes 1½ cups
1½ cups confectioners' sugar
¼ cup whole buttermilk
½ teaspoon vanilla extract

Preheat oven to 350°. Spray 2 (9x5-inch) loaf pans with baking spray. Line bottom of pans with parchment paper, and spray pans again.

Cakes: In a large bowl, beat Browned Butter and 2 cups sugar with a mixer at medium speed until fluffy, 3 to 4 minutes, stopping to scrape sides of bowl. Add eggs, one at a time, beating well after each addition.

In a medium bowl, whisk together flour, baking powder, 1 tablespoon cinnamon, and 1 teaspoon salt. In a small bowl, whisk together buttermilk and vanilla. Reduce mixer speed to low. Gradually add flour mixture to butter mixture alternately with buttermilk mixture, beginning and ending with flour mixture, beating just until combined after each addition.

In a small bowl, whisk together remaining ¼ cup sugar, remaining 2 tablespoons cinnamon, and remaining ½ teaspoon salt.

Spoon a thin layer of batter into prepared pans. Sprinkle with 2 tablespoons cinnamon mixture, covering entire surface of batter. Repeat process twice, ending with batter. Pull a wooden skewer through batter in a swirling pattern. Tap pans on counter to release any air bubbles.

Bake until a wooden pick inserted in center comes out clean, 55 minutes to 1 hour and 10 minutes. Let cool in pans for 10 minutes. Remove from pans, and let cool completely on a wire rack. Spoon Buttermilk Glaze over cakes. Garnish with pecans, if desired. Cover and refrigerate for up to 5 days.

Browned Butter: In a medium saucepan, cook butter over medium heat, stirring occasionally, until butter turns a medium-brown color and has a nutty aroma. Remove from heat, and strain through a fine-mesh sieve. Cover and refrigerate for up to 3 days. Bring to room temperature before using.

Buttermilk Glaze: In a small bowl, whisk together all ingredients until smooth. Use immediately.

Orange Cardamom Loaves

MAKES 2 (8X4-INCH) LOAVES

Cakes
2½ cups sugar
1½ cups whole milk
1 cup vegetable oil
3 large eggs
2 tablespoons orange zest
1½ teaspoons vanilla extract
3 cups all-purpose flour
1½ teaspoons salt
1½ teaspoons baking powder
¼ teaspoon ground cardamom
Orange Glaze (recipe follows)

Orange Glaze
Makes about 1⅓ cups
2 cups confectioners' sugar
1 teaspoon orange zest
⅓ cup fresh orange juice

Preheat oven to 350°. Spray 2 (8x4-inch) loaf pans with baking spray with flour.

Cakes: In a large bowl, beat sugar, milk, oil, eggs, zest, and vanilla with a mixer at medium speed until well combined.

In a medium bowl, sift together flour, salt, baking powder, and cardamom. Reduce mixer speed to low. Gradually add flour mixture to sugar mixture, beating until smooth. Spoon batter into prepared pans.

Bake for 30 minutes. Loosely cover with foil, and bake until a wooden pick inserted in center comes out clean, about 30 minutes more. Let cool in pans for 10 minutes. Remove from pans, and let cool completely on a wire rack.

Drizzle with Orange Glaze; let stand until set, about 20 minutes. Store in an airtight container for up to 3 days.

Orange Glaze: In a medium bowl, whisk together all ingredients until smooth.

Banana Pound Cakes with Peanut Butter Swirl

MAKES 2 (9X5-INCH) LOAVES

Cakes
- 1 cup unsalted butter, softened
- 1½ cups sugar
- 6 large eggs
- 3 cups all-purpose flour
- 1½ teaspoons baking powder
- 1 teaspoon baking soda
- 1 teaspoon sa lt
- 1½ cups mashed banana (about 3 large bananas)
- ½ cup sour cream
- 1 tablespoon vanilla extract
- Peanut Butter Swirl (recipe follows)
- Semisweet Chocolate Glaze (recipe follows)

Peanut Butter Swirl
- ½ (8-ounce) package cream cheese, softened
- ¼ cup creamy peanut butter
- ¼ cup sugar
- ¼ cup unsweetened cocoa powder
- 1 large egg
- 1 tablespoon all-purpose flour

Semisweet Chocolate Glaze
- ½ cup heavy whipping cream
- 1 cup semisweet chocolate morsels

Preheat oven to 325°. Spray 2 (9x5-inch) loaf pans with baking spray with flour.

Cakes: In a large bowl, beat butter and sugar with a mixer at medium speed until fluffy, 3 to 4 minutes, stopping to scrape sides of bowl. Add eggs, one at a time, beating well after each addition.

In a medium bowl, whisk together flour, baking powder, baking soda, and salt. Reduce mixer speed to low. Gradually add flour mixture to butter mixture, beating just until combined after each addition. Stir in mashed banana, sour cream, and vanilla.

Divide one-third of batter between prepared pans. Spoon half of Peanut Butter Swirl over batter in each pan, avoiding edges of pan. Repeat layers with remaining cake batter and Peanut Butter Swirl. Using a knife, swirl batter, being careful to not tuch sides of pan. Smooth tops using an offset spatula.

Bake until a wooden pick inserted in center comes out clean, about 1 hour. Let cool in pans for 15 minutes. Remove from pans, and let cool completely on wire racks. Drizzle Semisweet Chocolate Glaze over cooled cake. Serve immediately.

Peanut Butter Swirl: In a medium bowl, beat cream cheese, peanut butter, sugar, cocoa, egg, and flour with a mixer at medium speed until smooth.

Semisweet Chocolate Glaze: In a microwave-safe bowl, microwave cream for 1 minute. Add chocolate, stirring until smooth.

Sweet Tea Poke Pound Cakes with Lemon Glaze

MAKES 2 (8X4-INCH) LOAVES

Cakes

1⅔ cups whole milk
8 family-size tea bags, divided
2 cups unsalted butter, softened
4 cups sugar, divided
4 large eggs
2 teaspoons vanilla extract
4 cups all-purpose flour
1½ teaspoons salt
1 teaspoon baking powder
1 cup water
Lemon Glaze (recipe follows)
Garnish: lemon slices

Lemon Glaze

1 tablespoon lemon zest
¼ cup fresh lemon juice
2 tablespoons heavy whipping cream
1 tablespoon light corn syrup
½ cup granulated sugar
2 tablespoons unsalted butter
1¾ cups confectioners' sugar

cake tip

After pouring syrup mixture over loaves, you can freeze them for later use.

Preheat oven to 325°. Spray 2 (8x4-inch) loaf pans with baking spray with flour.

Cakes: In a small saucepan, bring milk and 4 tea bags to a simmer over medium heat, stirring frequently. Remove from heat, and let steep for 5 minutes. Press tea bags to release excess liquid; discard tea bags. Measure 1⅓ cups milk mixture. Refrigerate to let cool completely.

In a large bowl, beat 2 cups butter and 3 cups sugar with a mixer at medium speed until fluffy, 3 to 4 minutes, stopping to scrape sides of bowl. Add eggs, one at a time, beating well after each addition. Beat in vanilla.

In another large bowl, whisk together together flour, salt, and baking powder. Reduce mixer speed to low. Gradually add flour mixture to butter mixture alternately with milk mixture, beginning and ending with flour mixture, beating just until combined after each addition. Divide batter between prepared pans.

Bake until a wooden pick inserted in center comes out clean, about 1 hour and 35 minutes. Let cool in pans for 20 minutes.

In a small saucepan, bring 1 cup water, remaining 1 cup granulated sugar, and remaining 4 tea bags to a boil over medium-high heat. Remove from heat, and let steep for 5 minutes. Press tea bags to release excess liquid; discard tea bags. Let cool at room temperature.

Using a wooden skewer, poke holes in warm loaves. Carefully pour syrup mixture over loaves. Let cool completely. Pour Lemon Glaze over cooled loaves. Garnish with lemon slices, if desired.

Lemon Glaze: In a small saucepan, bring zest and juice, cream, corn syrup, granulated sugar, and butter to a boil over medium-high heat. Reduce heat to medium-low; cook for 1 minute. Remove from heat; add confectioners' sugar, and whisk for 1 minute. Let cool for 3 minutes.

Chocolate-Vanilla Swirl Pound Cake

MAKES 1 (8X4-INCH) LOAF

- ¼ cup bittersweet chocolate morsels
- ¾ cup unsalted butter, softened
- ½ (8-ounce) package cream cheese, softened
- 1 cup granulated sugar
- ½ cup firmly packed brown sugar
- 1 teaspoon vanilla extract
- 3 large eggs, room temperature
- 1½ cups all-purpose flour
- ½ teaspoon baking powder
- ⅛ teaspoon salt
- 2 tablespoons whole milk
- ¼ cup unsweetened cocoa powder

Preheat oven to 300°. Spray an 8x4-inch loaf pan with baking spray with flour.

In a small microwave-safe bowl, microwave chocolate morsels on medium in 30-second intervals, stirring between each, until chocolate is melted and smooth (about 1½ minutes total). Let stand until cool.

In a large bowl, beat butter and cream cheese with a mixer at medium speed until smooth. Add sugars and vanilla; beat until fluffy, 3 to 4 minutes, stopping to scrape sides of bowl. Add eggs, one at a time, beating well after each addition.

In a medium bowl, whisk together flour, baking powder, and salt. With mixer at low speed, gradually add flour mixture to butter mixture, beating until combined. Spoon 2 cups batter into a medium bowl; stir in milk. Add melted chocolate and cocoa to remaining batter in large bowl; beat until combined.

Alternately drop vanilla and chocolate batters by heaping tablespoonfuls into prepared pan; gently swirl batters together using the tip of a knife. Tap pan on counter twice to release any air bubbles.

Bake until a wooden pick inserted in center comes out clean, about 1 hour and 25 minutes. Let cool in pan for 30 minutes. Run a knife around edges of pan. Remove from pan, and let cool completely on wire rack.

Mini Pound Cakes

MAKES 7 (6X3-INCH) LOAVES

- 1 cup unsalted butter, softened
- 3 cups sugar
- 5 large eggs
- 1 cup low-fat vanilla yogurt
- ¼ cup heavy whipping cream
- ½ teaspoon vanilla extract
- 3½ cups cake flour*
- ¼ teaspoon salt
- ¼ teaspoon baking soda
- Jam, to serve

Preheat oven to 300°. Spray 7 (6x3-inch) miniature loaf pans with baking spray with flour.

In a large bowl, beat butter and sugar with a mixer at medium speed until fluffy, 3 to 4 minutes, stopping to scrape sides of bowl. Add eggs, one at a time, beating well after each addition. Beat in yogurt, cream, and vanilla.

In a medium bowl, whisk together flour, salt, and baking soda. Reduce mixer speed to low. Gradually add flour mixture to butter mixture, beating until combined. Divide batter among prepared pans.

Bake until a wooden pick inserted in center comes out clean, 35 to 45 minutes. Let cool in pans for 10 minutes. Run a knife around edges of pans to loosen cakes. Remove from pans, and let cool completely on wire racks. Serve with jam, if desired.

**We used Swans Down.*

Cinnamon Roll Pound Cake

MAKES 1 (10X5-INCH) LOAF

Cake
- ¾ cup unsalted butter, softened
- ½ cup butter-flavored shortening
- 2 cups granulated sugar
- 4 large eggs, room temperature
- 2¼ cups sifted cake flour
- 2 teaspoons baking powder
- 2 teaspoons ground cinnamon, divided
- 1 teaspoon salt
- ¾ cup sour cream
- ⅓ cup half-and-half
- 3 teaspoons vanilla extract, divided
- ⅓ cup firmly packed brown sugar
- ⅓ cup unsalted butter, melted
- 2 teaspoons all-purpose flour
- Cream Cheese Glaze (recipe follows)

Cream Cheese Glaze
Makes about 1½ cups
- 1 (8-ounce) package cream cheese, softened
- ½ cup confectioners' sugar
- ¼ cup heavy whipping cream
- ½ teaspoon vanilla extract

Preheat oven to 325°. Spray a 10x5-inch loaf pan with baking spray with flour; line bottom of pan with parchment paper.

Cake: In a large bowl, beat butter, shortening, and granulated sugar with a mixer at medium speed until fluffy, 3 to 4 minutes, stopping to scrape sides of bowl. Add eggs, one at a time, beating well after each addition.

In a medium bowl, whisk together cake flour, baking powder, 1 teaspoon cinnamon, and salt. In a small bowl, whisk together sour cream, half-and-half, and 2 teaspoons vanilla. Reduce mixer speed to low. Gradually add flour mixture to butter mixture alternately with sour cream mixture, beginning and ending with flour mixture, beating just until combined after each addition.

In a small bowl, whisk together brown sugar, melted butter, all-purpose flour, remaining 1 teaspoon cinnamon, and remaining 1 teaspoon vanilla.

Spoon one-fourth of batter into prepared pan. Sprinkle one-fourth of cinnamon sugar mixture over batter. Pull a knife through batter to create a swirl pattern. Repeat procedure three times, alternating batter and cinnamon sugar mixture, swirling after each addition.

Bake until a wooden pick inserted in center comes out clean, about 1 hour and 15 minutes, covering with foil halfway through baking to prevent excess browning. Let cool in pan for 10 minutes. Remove from pan, and let cool completely on a wire rack. Drizzle Cream Cheese Glaze over cooled cake. Store covered at room temperature for up to 3 days.

Cream Cheese Glaze: In a medium bowl, beat cream cheese and confectioners' sugar with a mixer at medium speed until smooth, about 3 minutes. With mixer at medium-high speed, add cream and vanilla, beating until smooth. Use immediately.

Coconut Pound Cake

MAKES 1 (9X5-INCH) LOAF

Cake
- ¾ cup unsalted butter, softened
- ½ (8-ounce) package cream cheese, softened
- 1½ cups sugar
- 3 large eggs
- 2 teaspoons vanilla extract
- 1 teaspoon coconut extract
- 1½ cups all-purpose flour
- 1 teaspoon salt
- ½ teaspoon baking powder
- ½ teaspoon lemon zest

Coconut Glaze (recipe follows)
Garnish: fresh coconut shavings

Coconut Glaze
Makes 1 cup
- 2 cups confectioners' sugar
- ¼ cup unsweetened coconut milk
- 1 tablespoon fresh lemon juice

Preheat oven to 350°. Spray a 9x5-inch loaf pan with baking spray with flour.

Cake: In the bowl of a stand mixer fitted with the paddle attachment, beat butter and cream cheese at medium speed until smooth. Add sugar, and beat until fluffy, 3 to 4 minutes, stopping to scrape sides of bowl. Add eggs, one at a time, beating well after each addition. Beat in extracts.

In a medium bowl, stir together flour, salt, baking powder, and zest. Reduce mixer speed to low. Gradually add flour mixture to butter mixture, beating just until combined. Spoon batter into prepared pan.

Bake until a wooden pick inserted in center comes out clean, about 1 hour and 5 minutes. Let cool in pan for 10 minutes. Remove from pan, and let cool completely on a wire rack. Pour Coconut Glaze over cooled cake. Garnish with coconut shavings, if desired.

Coconut Glaze: In a small bowl, whisk together confectioners' sugar, coconut milk, and juice until smooth. Use immediately.

Glazed Lemon, Poppy Seed, and Thyme Cakes

MAKES 2 (8X4-INCH) LOAVES

Cakes
- 2 cups unsalted butter, softened
- 2 cups sugar
- 2 tablespoons poppy seeds
- 2 tablespoons chopped fresh thyme
- 4 large eggs, room temperature
- 1½ cups all-purpose flour
- 1½ cups cake flour
- 1 teaspoon baking powder
- ¼ teaspoon salt
- 1 cup whole buttermilk, room temperature
- 1 teaspoon lemon zest
- 2 tablespoons fresh lemon juice
- 1 teaspoon vanilla extract
- Lemon Glaze (recipe follows)
- Garnish: fresh thyme, lemon slices

Lemon Glaze
Makes about 1¼ cups
- 1 cup confectioners' sugar
- ¼ cup fresh lemon juice

Preheat oven to 350°. Spray 2 (8x4-inch) loaf pans with baking spray with flour.

Cakes: In a large bowl, beat butter and sugar with a mixer at medium speed until creamy, 3 to 4 minutes, stopping to scrape sides of bowl. Add poppy seeds and thyme, beating until combined. Add eggs, one at a time, beating well after each addition.

In another large bowl, sift together flours, baking powder, and salt. In a small bowl, whisk together buttermilk, zest, juice, and vanilla. Reduce mixer speed to low. Gradually add flour mixture to butter mixture alternately with buttermilk mixture, beginning and ending with flour mixture, beating just until combined after each addition. Divide batter between prepared pans.

Bake for 30 minutes. Cover with foil, and bake until a wooden pick inserted in center comes out clean, 30 to 45 minutes more. Let cool in pans for 10 minutes. Remove from pans, and let cool completely on a wire rack. Pour Lemon Glaze over cooled loaves. Garnish with thyme and lemon slices, if desired.

Lemon Glaze: In a small bowl, whisk together confectioners' sugar and lemon juice until smooth. Use immediately.

Strawberry Cream Cheese Pound Cake, page 230

Peach Cobbler Pound Cake

MAKES 1 (9X5-INCH) LOAF

Cake
½ cup unsalted butter, softened
1¼ cups sugar
3 large eggs, room temperature
2 cups plus 2 tablespoons all-purpose flour, divided
½ teaspoon salt
¼ teaspoon baking powder
½ cup whole buttermilk, room temperature
1½ teaspoons vanilla extract
1 cup chopped fresh peaches
⅓ cup roughly chopped pecan pralines*
Cobbler Crumbs (recipe follows)
Praline Sauce (recipe follows), to serve

Cobbler Crumbs
½ cup all-purpose flour
2 tablespoons sugar
½ teaspoon ground cinnamon
¼ cup cold unsalted butter, cubed

Praline Sauce
⅔ cup firmly packed brown sugar
⅓ cup unsalted butter
¾ cup chopped toasted pecans
⅔ cup heavy whipping cream
1 teaspoon vanilla extract

Preheat oven to 325°. Spray a 9x5-inch loaf pan with baking spray with flour. Line pan with parchment paper, letting excess extend over sides of pan.

Cake: In the bowl of a stand mixer fitted with the paddle attachment, beat butter and sugar at medium speed until light and fluffy, 3 to 4 minutes, stopping to scrape sides of bowl. Add eggs, one at a time, beating well after each addition.

In a medium bowl, whisk together 2 cups flour, salt, and baking powder. In a small bowl, stir together buttermilk and vanilla. With mixer on low speed, gradually add flour mixture to butter mixture alternately with buttermilk mixture, beginning and ending with flour mixture, beating just until combined after each addition.

In another medium bowl, toss together peaches and remaining 2 tablespoons flour to coat. Gently fold peaches, pralines, and baked Cobbler Crumbs into batter. Spoon batter into prepared pan, leveling as needed. Firmly tap pan on a counter 5 to 7 times to level batter and release any air bubbles. Top with unbaked Cobbler Crumbs.

Bake until a wooden pick inserted in center comes out clean and an instant-read thermometer inserted in center registers at least 205°, about 1 hour and 30 minutes. Let cool in pan for 15 minutes. Using excess parchment as handles, remove from pan, and let cool completely on a wire rack. Serve with Praline Sauce.

Cobbler Crumbs: In a medium bowl, whisk together flour, sugar, and cinnamon. Using a pastry blender or 2 forks, cut in cold butter until mixture is crumbly and butter is incorporated. Refrigerate until cold and firm, at least 30 minutes.

Preheat oven to 350°. Line a small rimmed baking sheet with parchment paper. Spread half of flour mixture onto prepared pan. (Leave remaining half unbaked.)

Bake until golden brown and crisp, 15 to 20 minutes. Let cool completely. Crumble baked crumbs into pieces.

Praline Sauce: In a medium saucepan, melt brown sugar and butter over medium heat, stirring occasionally. Stir in pecans, and cook for 30 seconds to 1 minute. Reduce heat to low, and carefully stir in cream. Increase heat to medium, and cook, stirring constantly, until thickened, 2 to 3 minutes. Remove from heat, and stir in vanilla. Let stand for 10 minutes.

**We used Cane River Pecan Co. Pralines.*

Blackberry Buttermilk Pound Cakes

MAKES 2 (8X4-INCH) LOAVES

Cakes
- 1½ cups unsalted butter, softened
- 3 cups sugar
- 6 large eggs, room temperature
- 1 teaspoon vanilla extract
- 3 cups all-purpose flour
- ⅛ teaspoon baking soda
- ¾ cup whole buttermilk
- 2 cups fresh blackberries, divided
- Blackberry Jam Glaze (recipe follows)

Blackberry Jam Glaze
- 2 cups confectioners' sugar
- 6 tablespoons heavy whipping cream
- 2 tablespoons seedless blackberry jam

Preheat oven to 325°. Spray 2 (8x4-inch) loaf pans with baking spray with flour.

Cakes: In a large bowl, beat butter and sugar with a mixer at medium speed until fluffy, 3 to 4 minutes, stopping to scrape sides of bowl. Add eggs, one at a time, beating well after each addition. Beat in vanilla.

In a medium bowl, whisk together flour and baking soda. With mixer at low speed, gradually add flour mixture to butter mixture alternately with buttermilk, beginning and ending with flour mixture, beating just until combined after each addition. Fold in 1 cup blackberries. Divide batter between prepared pans.

Bake for 20 minutes. Sprinkle with remaining 1 cup blackberries, and bake until browned and a wooden pick inserted in center comes out clean, 40 to 50 minutes more. Let cool completely in pans. Remove from pans. Pour Blackberry Jam Glaze over cooled cakes.

Blackberry Jam Glaze: In a small bowl, whisk together confectioners' sugar, cream, and jam.

Lemon-Cornmeal Pound Cakes

MAKES 2 (9X5-INCH) LOAVES

Cakes
- 2 cups unsalted butter, softened
- 2 cups sugar
- 3 cups all-purpose flour
- ½ cup plain yellow cornmeal
- 1 teaspoon baking powder
- ½ teaspoon salt
- 6 large eggs
- 1 teaspoon vanilla extract
- 3 teaspoons lemon zest, divided
- 1 cup whole milk

Lemon Glaze (recipe follows)
Fresh peach slices and sweetened whipped cream, to serve

Lemon Glaze
- 2 cups confectioners' sugar
- 2 tablespoons fresh lemon juice
- 4 to 6 tablespoons whole milk

Preheat oven to 325°. Spray 2 (9x5-inch) loaf pans with baking spray with flour.

Cakes: In a large bowl, beat butter and sugar with a mixer at medium speed until creamy, 3 to 4 minutes, stopping to scrape sides of bowl. In a medium bowl, combine flour, cornmeal, baking powder, and salt; stir well. Add eggs, one at a time, beating well after each addition. Add vanilla and 1 teaspoon zest, beating just until combined.

Reduce mixer speed to low. Gradually add flour mixture to butter mixture alternately with milk, beginning and ending with flour mixture, beating just until combined after each addition. (Batter will be thick.) Divide batter between prepared pans.

Bake until a wooden pick inserted in center comes out clean, 1 hour to 1 hour and 5 minutes. Let cool in pans for 10 minutes. Remove from pans, and let cool completely on a wire rack.

Drizzle Lemon Glaze over cakes, and sprinkle with remaining 2 teaspoons zest. Serve with peaches and whipped cream.

Lemon Glaze: In a small bowl, whisk together confectioners' sugar, lemon juice, and 2 tablespoons milk until smooth, adding remaining milk to achieve a thin consistency, if necessary.

Sweet Potato-Cream Cheese Pound Cakes

MAKES 2 (9X5-INCH) LOAVES

- 1 (8-ounce) package cream cheese, softened
- ½ cup unsalted butter, softened
- 1 cup firmly packed brown sugar
- 1 cup granulated sugar
- 4 large eggs
- 1½ cups peeled grated sweet potato
- 1 teaspoon vanilla extract
- 3 cups self-rising flour
- 1½ teaspoons pumpkin pie spice

Preheat oven to 350°. Spray 2 (9x5-inch) loaf pans with baking spray with flour.

In a large bowl, beat cream cheese and butter with a mixer at medium speed until creamy. Add sugars; beat until fluffy, 3 to 4 minutes, stopping to scrape sides of bowl. Add eggs, one at a time, beating well after each addition. Add sweet potato and vanilla, beating until combined.

In a medium bowl, whisk together flour and pumpkin pie spice. Reduce mixer speed to low. Gradually add flour mixture to sweet potato mixture, beating just until combined. Divide batter between prepared pans.

Bake until a wooden pick inserted in center comes out clean, about 45 minutes. Let cool in pans 10 minutes. Remove from pans, and let cool completely on a wire rack.

Skillet Pound Cake with Peaches

MAKES 1 (10-INCH) CAKE

Cake

- 1 cup unsalted butter, softened
- 1 cup granulated sugar
- 4 large eggs, room temperature
- 1 teaspoon vanilla extract
- 2 cups all-purpose flour
- 1 teaspoon baking powder
- ¼ teaspoon salt
- 2 tablespoons confectioners' sugar
- Peach Topping (recipe follows)

Peach Topping

- ½ cup granulated sugar
- ½ cup water
- ⅛ teaspoon salt
- 1 tablespoon fresh lemon juice
- ½ teaspoon vanilla extract
- 4 cups sliced fresh peaches
- 2 tablespoons chopped fresh mint

Preheat oven to 325°.

Cake: In a large bowl, beat butter and granulated sugar with a mixer at medium speed until creamy, 3 to 4 minutes, stopping to scrape sides of bowl. Add eggs, one at a time, beating well after each addition. Beat in vanilla.

In a medium bowl, whisk together flour, baking powder, and salt. With mixer at low speed, gradually add flour mixture to butter mixture, beating until combined. Spoon batter into a 10-inch cast-iron skillet, smoothing top with an offset spatula.

Bake until a wooden pick inserted in center comes out clean, about 35 minutes. Let cool completely on a wire rack. Sprinkle with confectioners' sugar. Serve with Peach Topping.

Peach Topping: In a small saucepan, bring sugar, ½ cup water, and salt to a boil over high heat. Cook for 1 minute. Remove from heat; stir in juice and vanilla. Pour into a medium bowl; let cool. Add peaches; cover and refrigerate for at least 2 hours or overnight. Stir in mint just before serving.

Vanilla Bean Pound Cakes

MAKES 2 (9X5 INCH) LOAVES

- ¾ cup unsalted butter, softened
- 1½ cups sugar
- 4 large eggs
- 1 vanilla bean, split lengthwise, seeds scraped and reserved
- 1½ teaspoons vanilla extract
- 1½ cups all-purpose flour
- ¼ teaspoon salt
- ½ cup heavy whipping cream
- Whipped cream and fresh berries, to serve
- Fresh berries, to serve

- Sweetened whipped cream and fresh berries, to serve

Preheat oven to 300°. Spray 2 (9x5-inch) loaf pans with baking spray with flour.

In a large bowl, beat butter and sugar with a mixer at medium speed until fluffy, 3 to 4 minutes, stopping to scrape sides of bowl. Add eggs, one at a time, beating well after each addition. Beat in vanilla bean seeds and vanilla extract.

In a medium bowl, sift together flour and salt. Reduce mixer speed to low. Gradually add flour mixture to butter mixture alternately with cream, beginning and ending with flour mixture, beating just until combined after each addition. Divide batter between prepared pans.

Bake for 1 hour. Cover loosely with foil, and bake until a wooden pick inserted in center comes out clean, 5 to 10 minutes more. Let cool in pans for 15 minutes. Remove from pans, and let cool completely on a wire rack. Serve with whipped cream and fresh berries.

Honey-Orange Loaf Pound Cakes

MAKES 4 (5X3-INCH) LOAVES

Cakes
- 1¾ cups cake flour
- 1 cup granulated sugar
- 2 teaspoons baking powder
- ¼ teaspoon salt
- ½ cup vegetable oil
- ½ cup fresh orange juice
- 2 tablespoons honey
- 4 large egg whites
- 2 tablespoons confectioners' sugar

Orange Glaze (recipe follows)

Orange Glaze
Makes about 2 cups
- 2 cups confectioners' sugar
- ¼ cup fresh orange juice
- 2 tablespoons honey

Preheat oven to 350°. Spray 4 (5x3-inch) loaf pans with baking spray with flour.

Cakes: In a large bowl, sift together flour, granulated sugar, baking powder, and salt. Add oil, orange juice, and honey, whisking until smooth.

In a small bowl, beat egg whites with a mixer at high speed until soft peaks form. Gradually add confectioners' sugar, beating until stiff peaks form. Gently fold into batter. Divide batter among prepared pans.

Bake until a wooden pick inserted in center comes out clean, 20 to 25 minutes. Let cool in pans for 10 minutes. Remove from pans, and let cool completely on a wire rack. Pour Orange Glaze over cakes.

Orange Glaze: In a large bowl, whisk together confectioners' sugar, orange juice, and honey until smooth.

Enjoy!
Enjoy!

Strawberry Shortcake Pound Cake

MAKES 1 (10X5 INCH) LOAF

1 cup unsalted butter, softened
2 cups sugar
5 large eggs
1 tablespoon strawberry extract
½ teaspoon vanilla extract
2¼ cups all-purpose flour
½ teaspoon salt
1 cup chopped fresh strawberries
½ cup sour cream
Sliced fresh strawberries, strawberry syrup, and sweetened whipped cream, to serve
Garnish: toasted chopped almonds, fresh mint sprigs

Preheat oven to 350°. Spray a 10x5-inch loaf pan with baking spray with flour.

In a large bowl, beat butter and sugar with a mixer at medium speed until fluffy, 3 to 4 minutes, stopping to scrape sides of bowl. Add eggs, one at a time, beating well after each addition. Beat in extracts.

In a medium bowl, whisk together flour and salt. Reduce mixer speed to low. Gradually add flour mixture to butter mixture, beating just until combined. Stir in chopped strawberries and sour cream. Spoon batter into prepared pan.

Bake for 1 hour. Cover loosely with foil, and bake until a wooden pick inserted in center comes out clean, 40 to 45 minutes more. Let cool in pan for 10 minutes. Remove from pan, and let cool completely on a wire rack. Serve with sliced strawberries, strawberry syrup, and whipped cream. Garnish with almonds and mint, if desired.

Strawberry Cream Cheese Pound Cakes

MAKES 2 (8X4-INCH) LOAVES

Cakes
1 (8-ounce) package cream cheese, softened
1 cup unsalted butter, softened
3 cups sugar
6 large eggs
1 tablespoon vanilla extract
3½ cups all-purpose flour
¼ teaspoon baking powder
½ teaspoon salt
1 cup heavy whipping cream
Strawberry Sauce (recipe follows)
Fresh strawberries and sweetened whipped cream, to serve

Strawberry Sauce
Makes about 1 cup
1 pint fresh strawberries
2 tablespoons water
1 tablespoon cornstarch
3 tablespoons sugar

Preheat oven to 325°. Spray 2 (8x4-inch) loaf pans with baking spray with flour.

Cakes: In a large bowl, beat cream cheese and butter with a mixer at medium speed until creamy. Add sugar; beat until fluffy, 3 to 4 minutes, stopping to scrape sides of bowl. Add eggs, one at a time, beating well after each addition. Beat in vanilla.

In another large bowl, sift together flour, baking powder, and salt. Reduce mixer speed to low. Gradually add flour mixture to butter mixture alternately with cream, beginning and ending with flour mixture, beating just until combined after each addition. Transfer half of batter to a medium bowl; set aside.

Spoon one-third of remaining batter into one prepared pan. Place ¼ cup Strawberry Sauce in center of batter. Repeat layers once; top with remaining one-third of batter. Using a wooden skewer, gently swirl batter. Repeat process in remaining pan with remaining batter and remaining Strawberry Sauce. Tap pans on counter twice to release air bubbles.

Bake until a wooden pick inserted in center comes out clean, about 1 hour and 10 minutes. Let cool in pans for 10 minutes. Remove from pans, and let cool completely on a wire rack. Serve with strawberries and whipped cream.

Strawberry Sauce: In the work bowl of a food processor, pulse strawberries until smooth, about 1 minute.

In a small bowl, whisk together 2 tablespoons water and cornstarch until smooth.

In a medium saucepan, heat puréed strawberries and sugar over medium-high heat. Whisk in cornstarch mixture. Bring to a boil; cook, stirring constantly, until thickened, about 1 minute.

Coffee Pound Cake

MAKES 1 (9X5-INCH) LOAF

Cake
- 3 tablespoons espresso powder
- 1 tablespoon warm water
- ½ cup whole milk
- 1 cup unsalted butter, softened
- 1¼ cups sugar
- 1 teaspoon vanilla extract
- 3 large eggs
- 1¾ cups all-purpose flour
- ½ teaspoon baking powder
- ¼ teaspoon salt
- Espresso-Vanilla Syrup (recipe follows), to serve
- Espresso Whipped Cream (recipe follows), to serve

Espresso-Vanilla Syrup
- 1 tablespoon espresso powder
- 1 tablespoon warm water
- 1 cup water
- 1 cup granulated sugar
- 1 tablespoon dark corn syrup
- 1 (3-inch) vanilla bean, split lengthwise, seeds scraped and reserved

Espresso Whipped Cream
- 2½ teaspoons espresso powder
- 1½ teaspoons warm water
- 1 cup heavy whipping cream
- ¼ cup confectioners' sugar
- ½ teaspoon vanilla extract

Preheat oven to 300°. Spray a 9x5-inch cast-iron or metal loaf pan with baking spray with flour.

Cake: In a small bowl, whisk together espresso powder and 1 tablespoon warm water until dissolved. Add milk, stirring until combined.

In a large bowl, beat butter, sugar, and vanilla with a mixer at medium speed until fluffy, 3 to 4 minutes, stopping to scrape sides of bowl. Add eggs, one at a time, beating well after each addition.

In a medium bowl, whisk together flour, baking powder, and salt. With mixer on low speed, gradually add flour mixture to butter mixture, alternately with espresso mixture, beginning and ending with flour mixture, beating just until combined after each addition. Spoon batter into prepared pan. Tap pan twice on counter to release air bubbles.

Bake until a wooden pick inserted in center comes out clean, about 1 hour and 10 minutes. Let cool in pan for 30 minutes. Run a knife around edge of pan. Remove from pan, and let cool completely on a wire rack. Serve cake with Espresso-Vanilla Syrup and Espresso Whipped Cream.

Espresso-Vanilla Syrup: In a small bowl, whisk together espresso powder and 1 tablespoon warm water until dissolved.

In a small saucepan, bring 1 cup water, granulated sugar, and corn syrup to a boil over medium-high heat. Boil until mixture begins to become thick and syrupy, 8 to 10 minutes. Remove from heat. Stir in vanilla bean seeds and espresso mixture, stirring until combined. Let cool completely.

Espresso Whipped Cream: In a medium bowl, whisk together espresso powder and 1½ teaspoons warm water until espresso is dissolved. With a mixer at high speed, add cream, confectioners' sugar, and vanilla, beating until soft peaks form.

Fig Pound
Cake Crumb
Bars, page 248

Pound Cake with Berries and Nectarines

MAKES 1 (9X5 INCH) LOAF

- 3 large eggs
- ¼ cup whole milk
- 2 teaspoons vanilla extract
- 1½ cups cake flour
- ¾ cup sugar
- 1 teaspoon baking powder
- ¼ teaspoon salt
- ¾ cup unsalted butter, softened
- 4 cups sliced fresh nectarines
- 1 cup fresh blackberries
- 1 cup fresh blueberries
- ¼ cup honey
- 2 tablespoons almond-flavored liqueur
- 1 teaspoon orange zest
- Garnish: sweetened whipped cream

Preheat oven to 350°. Spray a 9x5-inch loaf pan with baking spray with flour.

In a medium bowl, whisk together eggs, milk, and vanilla. In a large bowl, stir together flour, sugar, baking powder, and salt. Add butter and half of egg mixture to flour mixture; beat with a mixer at low speed until combined. Increase mixer speed to medium-high; beat until fluffy, about 1 minute. Scrape sides of bowl, and add remaining egg mixture, ¼ cup at a time, beating well after each addition. Spoon batter into prepared pan, smoothing top with an offset spatula.

Bake until a wooden pick inserted in center comes out clean, about 1 hour. Let cool in pan for 10 minutes. Remove from pan, and let cool completely on a wire rack.

In a medium bowl, stir together nectarines, berries, honey, liqueur, and zest. Let stand for 5 minutes. Serve over pound cake. Garnish with whipped cream, if desired.

Chocolate-Graham Pound Cake

MAKES 1 (10-INCH) CAKE

Cake

- 1 cup plus 2 tablespoons unsalted butter, softened and divided
- ½ cup firmly packed brown sugar
- ½ cup granulated sugar
- 3 large eggs
- 1 teaspoon vanilla extract
- 1½ cups all-purpose flour
- 1 cup finely ground graham cracker crumbs
- 1 teaspoon baking powder
- ½ teaspoon salt, divided
- ⅔ cup full-fat sour cream
- 1 (7.5-ounce) jar marshmallow crème
- 1½ cups confectioners' sugar
- Chocolate Glaze (recipe follows)

Chocolate Glaze

- ¼ cup unsweetened cocoa powder
- 3 cups confectioners' sugar
- 6 tablespoons whole milk

Preheat oven to 325°. Spray a 10-inch cast-iron skillet with baking spray with flour.

Cake: In a large bowl, beat 1 cup butter and sugars with a mixer at medium speed until fluffy, about 3 minutes, stopping to scrape sides of bowl. Add eggs, one at a time, beating well after each addition. Beat in vanilla.

In a medium bowl, whisk together flour, graham cracker crumbs, baking powder, and ¼ teaspoon salt. With mixer at low speed, gradually add flour mixture to butter mixture alternately with sour cream, beginning and ending with flour mixture, beating just until combined after each addition. Spoon batter into prepared pan.

Bake until a wooden pick inserted in center comes out clean, about 45 minutes. Let cool in pan for 15 minutes. Remove from pan, and let cool completely on a wire rack. Place rack on a large rimmed baking sheet.

In a large bowl, beat marshmallow crème, remaining 2 tablespoons butter, and remaining ¼ teaspoon salt with a mixer at medium speed until smooth. (Crème will collapse.) With mixer at low speed, gradually add confectioners' sugar, beating until well combined. Increase mixer speed to medium, and beat for 1 minute.

Using a serrated knife, cut cake in half horizontally. Remove top half of cake; set aside. Spread marshmallow mixture onto bottom half of cake, leaving a 1-inch border. Cover with top half of cake. Freeze for 20 minutes. Pour Chocolate Glaze over cake, completely coating top and sides. Let stand until glaze is set, about 30 minutes. Transfer to a serving platter. Store covered and refrigerated for up to 2 days.

Chocolate Glaze: In a medium bowl, sift together cocoa and confectioners' sugar. Slowly whisk in milk until smooth.

Baby Carrot Pound Cakes

MAKES 4 INDIVIDUAL TIERED CAKES

Cakes
1½ cups unsalted butter, softened
1½ cups superfine sugar
6 large eggs
1½ teaspoons vanilla extract
1 teaspoon lemon zest
2¾ cups plus 2 tablespoons sifted cake flour
1 tablespoon baking powder
½ teaspoon ground ginger
¼ teaspoon salt
1⅓ cups shredded baby carrots, squeezed dry
Pourable Cream Cheese Frosting (recipe follows)
Garnish: carrot rosettes, fresh mint

Pourable Cream Cheese Frosting
Makes 6 to 7 cups
2 (8-ounce) packages cream cheese, softened
1¼ cups warm water
¾ cup powdered milk
1½ teaspoons clear vanilla extract
5 cups confectioners' sugar
Apricot food coloring paste

Preheat oven to 325°. Spray a 4-well multi-tier cake pan with baking spray with flour.

Cakes: In a large bowl, beat butter and superfine sugar with a mixer at medium speed until creamy, 3 to 4 minutes, stopping to scrape sides of bowl. Add eggs, one at a time, beating well after each addition. Beat in vanilla and zest.

In a medium bowl, sift together flour, baking powder, ginger, and salt. Reduce mixer speed to low. Gradually add flour mixture to butter mixture, beating just until combined. Gently fold in carrots. Divide batter among prepared wells. Tap pan on counter to release any air bubbles.

Bake until golden brown and a wooden pick inserted in center comes out clean, about 45 minutes. Let cool in pan for 5 minutes. Remove from pan, and let cool completely on a wire rack. Pour Pourable Cream Cheese Frosting over each cake to coat. Let dry, and coat again. Garnish with carrot rosettes and mint, if desired.

Pourable Cream Cheese Frosting: In a large bowl, beat cream cheese with a mixer at medium-high speed until smooth. Add 1¼ cups warm water, powdered milk, and vanilla, beating until combined. Gradually add confectioners' sugar, 1 cup at a time, beating until desired consistency is reached. Add a small amount of food coloring until desired color is reached.

cake tip

Apricot food coloring paste is available at cake-decorating supply stores.

Jo's Whipping Cream Pound Cakes

MAKES 12 CAKES

- 1 cup unsalted butter
- 3 cups sugar
- 5 large eggs
- 1½ teaspoons vanilla extract
- 3 cups cake flour
- 1 cup heavy whipping cream

Garnish: confectioners' sugar, sliced fresh strawberries

Preheat oven to 325°. Spray 12 (1½-cup) ramekins with baking spray with flour.

In a large bowl, beat butter and granulated sugar with a mixer at medium speed until fluffy, 3 to 4 minutes, stopping to scrape sides of bowl. Add eggs, one at a time, beating well after each addition. Beat in vanilla.

Reduce mixer speed to low. Gradually add flour to butter mixture alternately with cream, beginning and ending with flour, beating just until combined after each addition. Divide batter among prepared ramekins.

Bake until a wooden pick inserted in center comes out clean, 30 to 35 minutes. Let cool completely on a wire rack. Garnish with confectioners' sugar and strawberries, if desired.

Orange-Cream Cheese Pound Cakes

MAKES 12 CAKES

- 1 (8-ounce) package cream cheese, softened
- 1 cup unsalted butter, softened
- 2¼ cups sugar, divided
- 4 large eggs
- 2 tablespoons orange zest
- 3 tablespoons fresh orange juice
- 2¼ cups all-purpose flour
- 1 teaspoon baking powder
- ½ teaspoon salt
- ½ teaspoon ground cardamom
- 2 oranges, peeled and thinly sliced

Preheat oven to 325°. Spray 12 (1½-cup) ramekins with baking spray with flour.

In the bowl of a stand mixer fitted with the paddle attachment, beat cream cheese and butter at medium speed until creamy. Add 1½ cups sugar; beat until fluffy, 3 to 4 minutes, stopping to scrape sides of bowl. Add eggs, one at a time, beating well after each addition. Beat in zest and juice.

In a medium bowl, whisk together flour, baking powder, salt, and cardamom. Reduce mixer speed to low. Gradually add flour mixture to butter mixture, beating just until combined. Spoon batter into prepared ramekins, filling each three-fourths full.

Bake until a wooden pick inserted in center comes out clean, 30 to 35 minutes. Let cool completely in pans.

Just before serving, arrange orange slices over cooled cakes. Sprinkle with remaining ¾ cup sugar (about 1 tablespoon each). Using a kitchen torch, caramelize oranges. Serve immediately.

Bittersweet Mini Bundt Cakes with Brandied Whipped Cream

MAKES 6 CAKES

Cakes
- ¼ cup unsweetened cocoa powder
- ¼ cup boiling water
- 2 teaspoons espresso powder or instant coffee
- 1 cup unsalted butter
- ⅔ cup granulated sugar
- ⅔ cup firmly packed brown sugar
- 1½ teaspoons vanilla extract
- 3 large eggs
- 1⅔ cups all-purpose flour
- 1 teaspoon baking powder
- ½ teaspoon salt
- 2 ounces bittersweet chocolate, melted and cooled
- Bittersweet Chocolate Glaze (recipe follows)
- Brandied Whipped Cream (recipe follows), to serve
- Garnish: ground cinnamon

Bittersweet Chocolate Glaze
- 1 (4-ounce) bar bittersweet chocolate, finely chopped
- ½ cup heavy whipping cream
- ½ teaspoon vanilla extract

Brandied Whipped Cream
- 1 cup heavy whipping cream
- 2 tablespoons confectioners' sugar
- 2 tablespoons brandy
- ½ teaspoon vanilla extract

Preheat oven to 325°. Spray a 6-mold miniature fluted tube pan* with baking spray with flour.

Cakes: In a small bowl, whisk together cocoa, ¼ cup boiling water, and espresso powder until smooth. Let stand until cooled to room temperature.

In a large bowl, beat butter, sugars, and vanilla with a mixer at medium speed until fluffy, 3 to 4 minutes, stopping to scrape sides of bowl. Add eggs, one at a time, beating well after each addition.

In a medium bowl, whisk together flour, baking powder, and salt. Reduce mixer speed to low. Gradually add flour mixture and cocoa mixture to butter mixture, beating until combined. Beat in melted chocolate. (Batter will be thick.) Spoon batter into prepared molds, smoothing tops using an offset spatula. Tap pan on counter twice to release air bubbles.

Bake until a wooden pick inserted near center comes out clean, about 25 minutes. Let cool in pan for 10 minutes. Remove from pan, and let cool on a wire rack for 30 minutes. Spoon warm Bittersweet Chocolate Glaze over cakes. Serve with Brandied Whipped Cream. Garnish with cinnamon, if desired.

Bittersweet Chocolate Glaze: Place chopped chocolate in a medium bowl. In a small saucepan, heat cream to a simmer over medium heat. Pour over chocolate, stirring until smooth. Whisk in vanilla. Use immediately.

Brandied Whipped Cream: In a medium bowl, beat cream, confectioners' sugar, brandy, and vanilla with a mixer at high speed until soft peaks form. Use immediately, or cover and refrigerate for up to 1 hour.

**We used Wilton Excelle Elite Mini Fluted Tube Pan.*

Fig Pound Cake Crumb Bars

MAKES 9 BARS

Cake Crumbles
- 2 cups unsalted butter, softened
- 3 cups granulated sugar
- 4 large eggs
- 2 teaspoons vanilla extract
- ½ teaspoon almond extract
- 4 cups all-purpose flour
- ¾ teaspoon salt
- ¼ teaspoon baking soda
- 1 cup whole milk

Bars
Cake Crumbles (recipe above)
- ⅓ cup salted butter, softened
- ½ cup firmly packed brown sugar
- ½ teaspoon ground cardamom
- 1½ cups fig preserves*
- 5 fresh figs, quartered

Garnish: confectioners' sugar

Preheat oven to 325°. Spray a 16-cup straight-sided metal tube pan or 2 (9x5-inch) metal loaf pans with baking spray with flour.

Cake Crumbles: In a large bowl, beat butter and granulated sugar with a mixer at medium speed until fluffy, 2 minutes, stopping to scrape sides of bowl. Add eggs, one at a time, beating well after each addition. Beat in extracts.

In another large bowl, whisk together flour, salt, and baking soda. With mixer at low speed, gradually add flour mixture to butter mixture alternately with milk, beginning and ending with flour mixture, beating just until combined after each addition. Spoon batter into prepared pan.

Bake until a wooden pick inserted near center comes out clean, about 1 hour and 30 minutes for tube pan and about 1 hour and 15 minutes for loaf pans. Let cool in pan for 15 minutes. Remove from pan, and let cool completely on a wire rack.

Increase oven temperature to 350°. Crumble pound cake to equal 4 cups (about 6 slices). Arrange pound cake crumbles on a rimmed baking sheet. Bake for 15 minutes. Stir, and bake 10 minutes more. Let cool.

Bars: Line an 8-inch square baking pan with parchment paper, letting excess extend over sides of pan; spray with baking spray with flour.

In a large bowl, beat toasted Cake Crumbles, butter, brown sugar, and cardamom with a mixer at medium speed until mixture starts to clump together. Press 3 cups crumble mixture into bottom of prepared pan.

Bake for 15 minutes. Spread fig preserves onto crumble mixture. Arrange fig quarters over preserves. Sprinkle with remaining crumble mixture.

Bake until golden brown and bubbly, 35 to 40 minutes more. Let cool completely on a wire rack. Using excess parchment as handles, remove from pan, and cut into bars. Garnish with confectioners' sugar, if desired.

**We used Stonewall Kitchen Fig & Ginger Jam.*

Mini Almond Bundt Cakes with Lavender Glaze

MAKES 12 CAKES

Cakes

- 2½ cups sugar
- 2 large eggs, room temperature
- 1½ cups whole milk, room temperature
- 2 teaspoons almond extract
- 2½ cups all-purpose flour
- 1 teaspoon baking powder
- ½ cup unsalted butter, melted

Lavender Glaze

- 1½ cups confectioners' sugar
- ¼ cup whole milk
- 1 teaspoon dried lavender buds

Preheat oven to 350°. Generously spray 2 (6-well) miniature Bundt cake pans with baking spray with flour.

Cakes: In the bowl of a stand mixer fitted with the paddle attachment, beat sugar and eggs at medium speed until well combined. Beat in milk and almond extract.

In a medium bowl, whisk together flour and baking powder. With mixer at low speed, gradually add flour mixture to sugar mixture, beating until well combined, stopping to scrape sides of bowl. Gradually add melted butter, beating until combined. Pour batter into prepared pans.

Bake until a wooden pick inserted near center comes out clean, 35 to 40 minutes. Let cool in pans for 10 minutes. Remove from pans, and let cool completely on wire racks. Pour about 1 tablespoon Lavender Glaze over each cake. Store cakes in an airtight container.

Lavender Glaze: In a small bowl, whisk together confectioners' sugar, milk, and lavender.

recipe index

Bundt Cakes

Loaves & Mini Cakes

Tube Cakes

Frostings & Toppings

Glazes

Miscellaneous

Sauces & Syrups

White Chocolate
Pound Cake, page 81

SWANS DOWN
CAKE FLOUR
MADE IN
U.S.A